Janet M little

TRUE STORY

My
Tears
Were
For
Her

JANET M LITTLE

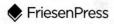 FriesenPress

Suite 300 - 990 Fort St
Victoria, BC, V8V 3K2
Canada

www.friesenpress.com

Author Webpage and Contact Info:
www.mytearswereforher.com

ISBN
978-1-5255-3401-0 (Hardcover)
978-1-5255-3402-7 (Paperback)
978-1-5255-3403-4 (eBook)

1. BIOGRAPHY & AUTOBIOGRAPHY

Distributed to the trade by The Ingram Book Company

Disclaimer:

This book is a factual depiction based on a true story of real events and was drawn from a variety of sources, including the author's personal journal materials and to the best of her ability, her own recollections, experiences, opinions, and views that are shared as truthfully as recollection permits and/or can be verified by research, and/or reports of which are documented, witnessed or both.

In some instances, quotes or dialogue consistent with the character or nature of the person speaking has also been drawn from memory and/or recollection to the best of the author's ability.

The opinions, recollections and views expressed in the book are those of the author only and do not necessarily reflect or represent the views and opinions held by individuals named or not named in the book.

Neither the author nor the publisher will be held liable or responsible for any actual or perceived loss or damage to any person or entity, caused or alleged to have been caused, directly or indirectly, by any information, views, opinions, suggestions, or any other content in this book. If you do not wish to be bound by the statements above, please know that you are entitled to not read this book.

Dedication

To you, the person who picked up this book, whose knees went weak and you felt sick to your stomach. You realize that this book has been written with you in mind. There is a plan and a purpose for you...

There is HOPE.

For any survivor of childhood sexual abuse who has kept "the secret" into adulthood, this book is for you as you embark on your healing journey. This is the journal of Janet's journey to take back her power and through her words encourages other survivors to do the same. Guilt and shame are the effects that are felt by survivors into adulthood and leaves us with feelings of helplessness and hopelessness. *My Tears Were for Her* reveals how forgiveness, therapy and journaling can free you from your past.

Brenda Campbell
Program Coordinator/Victim Support
Leduc & District Victim Services

Table of Contents

A Note from the Author

First, and most importantly, be aware that as an adult, you are obligated and expected to report any suspicions, knowledge or otherwise that you may have about any child known to you or not known to you that may be or is being abused, abandoned or maltreated. Failure to report may and can result in penalties.

For publishing and legal purposes, some names, much explicit language and what could prove to be traumatizing details have been removed. It is my belief that the explicit words (written in anger) that have been removed or replaced would only serve to take the focus away from the facts and the points being made and would deter some people from continuing to read to the end. I also believe that the detail remaining is enough to serve the purpose without being too graphic for some audiences. You as a reader might have your own details or don't need to be traumatized by the details of my particular story. The reason I share this is that I want you all to know that there were great outbursts of anger and extremely painful recollections of details that were experienced during this time. My intent is to leave as much as possible intact without taking away from the impact of my story.

Introduction

What you are about to read is a very real experience of disclosure. It contains detailed journal entries and diarized thoughts and actions that followed my initial admission of being a sexual abuse survivor. You will have access to the personal struggles, hardships and victories that I encountered when I made the decision to deal with the truth and fought to overcome it.

You may be thinking, *why would anyone do that?*

My purpose in sharing all of this is to let you and others know you are not alone. There is freedom in acknowledging and addressing your abuse. I know how shame held me back. I know there were many relationships in my life that I let go of, that I ran from to avoid getting too close, and others that I had no business being in.

My history was keeping me from my future.

So many women and men are locked up with the pain and shame of their sexual abuse, and they have no intention of dealing with it; they plan to take it all to the grave with them. If sharing my story can give courage to, or in some way encourage or influence even one person to seek the freedom and joy that exists on the other side of their painful past, then my purpose is complete.

I have been brought through this experience, healed, prepared, and equipped to share this and help others see light.

FEB. 20, '93

Breaking the Silence

Almost three weeks (Jan. 31) since I've broken the silence. It's like living in the twilight zone. I'm thirty-one years old now and just dealing with it. I guess I've dealt with it all my life, but alone. I'd like to keep this journal as a sign of hope so that I can look back as time passes and actually see the healing taking place rather than thinking it will never end.

Today was the second-worst day. The first one, I think, was telling Gord. It was so hard, but I had to. It was tell and take the chance of total destruction of our relationship, or not tell and let it self-destruct. Gord went out today and got this book for me so I could write. He doesn't think it's a big deal, but he has helped me more than he will ever know. His is the first unconditional love I think I've ever had.

Brad loves me too, I guess because I'm his sister, but I don't think there are any others. I'm not sure right now. Not people who are close to me, anyway. My friends, yes. Maybe I'm just putting "everyone" or saying "everyone" and actually meaning my father. Today I think he feels obligated to call it love for me so he could get away with the abuse. The love he now says he has for me is in all probability guilt. Maybe he's not even capable of feeling that.

The words are coming fast. Today in session, Susan compared my life in the family home to that of the POWs in concentration camps, which she described to me. Captors have total control and when afraid of rebellion, or to push their captives a little farther over the edge, they do something nice or give them something they want to twist their mind just a little bit more. Keep them wanting all the time and get what they want from them in the meantime. Earlier today the hatred, the pain, the total lack of respect I used to feel for him and about him came back. Now, tonight, it's turned to numbness. A no-feel, no-hurt presence.

I told Susan about Mom coming to the top of the stairs and calling Dad. We did discuss the fact that perhaps she was suspicious but did not want to face the truth. It's hard to think about now and feel hate for two people at once. Very mixed feelings about them both right now. Please, God, don't let the same thing have happened to Brad that happened to me. I don't know how I'll find out, but I have to. No other way but to ask when I get enough courage.

I left my family. I moved here to be with Gord and his family and now I feel I may have left them forever, permanently. As I saw my family then, I did. I think. I miss Brad now, terribly. Growing up there always seemed to be a rift between us, never real close, never talking about how we really felt; isolation I now believe was created by my father. Captors in camps, Susan explained, made sure of this so they could keep control. Today I remembered a lot of new things I had forgotten. I remember the abuse, vaguely, upstairs before I moved downstairs. I remember him leaving my room and me staring at that purple dresser until I'd fall asleep. No feelings attached. My eyes just focused on that dresser.

I remembered, too, making arrangements to leave the house—I would go and live with friends. My mother kept me from going. She cried and cried and talked me out of leaving. I must have been sixteen at the time. It was about then it ended. All of the verbal and physical abuse, hitting and punching him, must have been after it stopped or was my way of making it stop. I remember getting in trouble because they thought I was burning my hands with cigarettes and hiding them so they wouldn't see it. They were not cigarette burns. They were holes in my hands from suppressing anger. I dug the holes with my own fingernails.

How could I have lived such a nightmare and come out of it the way I did? I will be okay. I know that now.

I'll be better than I was six months ago. I will be fun to be with. I will be full of love and passion again. I will get through this a winner.

Gord doesn't realize it, but he is the most important thing in my life. I grieve and cry a lot lately for many reasons. The biggest thing I feel the last few days is the lost time we must suffer. Him and I. This isn't just me suffering. Gord will too. It just isn't fair. Why should he have to go through this? Why should he have to pay when he wasn't even around then? He thought he'd found the perfect happiness and now this. God is so cruel sometimes, but I think He is putting us through the ultimate test of love. Wants to see what we're really made of. He's going to find out. I've coped for thirty-one years alone, Gord has coped for twenty or maybe forty alone, so together, if we pool our strength, we can't be beat. We can only be better. I pray for that. Only better.

I grieve for a life that wasn't. I grieve for the child I never got to be. I grieve for my brother who has never really seemed to be truly happy. I grieve for my mother who seems to struggle at times, and sometimes I grieve my father who can't really like himself either. All the grieving hurts bad. The last time I remember grieving like this was when John was killed, and I locked myself inside my apartment for days with the lights off and the curtains closed. That was even not real because I took Valium to ease the pain. I still miss him and think about him a lot. John and I were very close friends and had been for many years. If you can say we grew up together at the tender age of 18, I am saying we did. One day we were together, the next he was gone. Just barely out of high school and he died in a vehicle accident. That was my first real tragedy.

I guess the grieving is part of healing. The book says it is good. I'm on my way. Hopefully it won't last long, because I can't control it. I can't turn off the feelings of grief on my "free days." Until I'm through it, I'll just have to accept that. The proper way to grieve is not to suppress it. Tomorrow is another day.

FEB. 22, '93

Self Worth and Secrets

I have a hard time accepting the fact that I can be loved with no strings attached. There are no conditions on the love Gord has for me. I've experienced that once before but was too caught up in dealing with the pain to love or realize I could be loved. I feel like I am a piece of entertainment. Sometimes a stereo or a game. I used to feel like this. My self-esteem is getting better, but I feel like I've always had to prove I was a person of worth. Not just to myself, but to everyone who knows me.

The pain of being abused by someone who had literally screwed my mind up badly, someone who I should have been able to turn to in times of trouble, has always affected me. I've never told Dad about things I was afraid of, rough times in my marriage or at work, or with substance abuse, or with alcohol. It was always Mom or a friend I would talk to. He would find a way to twist it or belittle it or make it sound like maybe it was my fault. The last two years I've told him much more because I always knew that (lately) if I didn't like his answer I could tell him to go to hell and I have. I've told him lots in the last few years about himself that he either denies or doesn't see. It seems easy now, but when the abuse was happening and up until the last while at home it was impossible. He overtook me, and I kept my mouth shut. I haven't quite figured out how or why yet, but he did.

I sometimes see him like a man without a life, trying to make up for the person he was for so many years. After the self-destructive time period, I was a workaholic. I had to prove myself and through my job was the only way. It was safe. I was in control. I am proud of the work I do and consider myself good at it. I am not, however, hiding in it any longer. By focusing on my job one hundred percent, I was rewarded well. My other relationships stunk, but I always had my job. No way was I ever going to be dependent upon anyone for anything. Thus, I had to earn a good living, live within my means and put away for the future. I have, I did, and I will continue to.

Dealing with difficult people is also a strength I've gained from this. Frustrating at times, but nothing could compare to what I did living there. No one could ever get to me like that again and no one would ever get full control of me again. I am independent, self-sufficient and proud of what I have accomplished. And now, as I learn more about the kind of person my father was then, I have to say that he did teach me to work hard and live within my means. Those are skills I can say he did teach me that have served me well.

Another good quality I have acquired is being a good listener. When you don't talk much about yourself everyone wants to tell you about themselves. I love it too. I take pride in being a good listener. And of course, I was good at keeping secrets. As you can well guess, secrets are not allowed in our home. There is such a thing as confidentiality between professionals or bonded people; however, in our books it is never okay to keep a secret that covers up anything that is immoral, illegal or hurtful to others. We agree that when used inappropriately, secrets hide the very evils that should be out in the open and not left producing more secrets and lies in the darkness. Children should never be asked to keep secrets about anything and should not be enabled by adults to keep them from the very people that can help them to deal with whatever they contain.

I realize that some of the ways I have coped over the years have been dangerous and very unhealthy, both physically and mentally. I can see when someone else has troubles and tells me about it that they are very real, and lots of times when I see people acting out in violence or anger, heavy drinking, substance abuse, and not talking, I always wonder what they are carrying around inside of them that they can't tell or have decided to pretend never happened. I'm sure some of their stories are very shocking as well.

FEB. 27, '93

How Could He?

How could he do that to a little girl, a young girl, a girl that was his own daughter, and then live in the same house and watch her get ugly inside and out?

How could he question my drinking? And preach and lecture about how alcohol is so bad and keep bottles stashed where he thought no one could find them? The only one he was fooling was himself and he was hurting everyone else around him. How could he do something so perverse to his own daughter and live the lie and tell me not to say anything to anyone?

How could she not suspect anything? After today's session I have to ask myself... was she abused too when she was young? Who knows. A mother who was would have to look after her own. So, I guess no is the answer to that. I've been wondering all day how I could help her if indeed she was abused. Susan said she had a chance to do something about it when it was happening to me if she was and if she suspected. Gord said if that's so, it wouldn't do any good to tell her now. If she did know, she did nothing about it. If she didn't know, it won't change anything. The little girl who suffered seems like someone else to me. It's as if I grieve for a little girl I know, but it wasn't me. It was me, and that I have a hard time with because there seems to be an open space between her and me. A space that somehow has a tie or connection but, in a way, I can't connect the two. It's confusing, and it's painful. It makes me sick.

Thursday, when I saw him, my father, and he mentioned no sex for a long time, I wanted to get up and kick him in the privates so it would be a lot longer before he had any. If I knew that he'd ever done that or would ever do it again, I'd hurt him. I don't think I could kill him, but I would hurt him in a way that he'd have to tell the truth. There would be no more lies. How could he make it seem to me that what happened was as much my fault as it was his? How does he make it look like I'm to blame, or anyone else, for that matter?

I wish my mom would have left him a long time ago. It's pretty hard to want kids when our childhood was one big cluster! I'm mad. I'm pissed off. I'm hurt, and I want to hurt him. It wouldn't do any good, though. No, Gord and I will sit here and work it out ourselves. Let them live in their own place. I wish Brad would move. It would be much healthier for him. If he could only get away long enough to realize that they are still trying to control his life. I'll tell him how nice it is. I only hope

Brad and his girlfriend are strong enough as a team to get out together.

Mom should have left when she had the chance. Maybe she still will. Maybe she too could realize what happiness and setting yourself free is all about. I'm leaving the hard way, the same way she'd have to, but I can see the bright light at the end of the tunnel. He'll just have to help himself.

MARCH 1, '93
Coping and Flashbacks

I remember using focusing to cope. I can still see every little animal on my dresser, every paint chip in the paint. Purple and white. Purple body and white handles, white trim. That dresser seems like a friend of mine. We spent lots of time staring at each other, feeling nothing.

Book covers... I would read them over and over and over and over again. I still do that. And I hate it. I see written words on books, the title, the author, and every time I enter that room I read it. Every time. And every time I do, I feel like moving it so I don't have to read it anymore, but I don't, and it gets me the very next time I go in that room.

I focused on the cracks in the cement wall, the different holes, the different shapes, many times through tears welling in my eyes, but I never cried so he could see me. Never. Never. When I used to dig the holes in the tops of my hand, it was like releasing the pressure in a pot that had built up so much it had to come out somehow. I couldn't scream in front of everyone, couldn't run wildly through the country pulling my hair out, I couldn't kill myself—that would hurt too many people's feelings—so I dug until blood came, and then, ashamed, I'd try to hide it. I'd do it and then I'd feel bad about it. I'm not sure why... maybe because I thought it was a stupid thing to do and so I was ashamed, terribly ashamed of what I'd done to myself. I used to think *you idiot, that's so stupid*, but kept doing it. It was like I couldn't help it.

Alcohol and substance abuse were rampant as I got older. I'm not sure and haven't associated yet fully why— whether it was easier for me to talk to other people, form relationships or what. I know that I used to have a terrible need to feel wanted. Getting drunk or medicating helped to ease the process of finding someone to be with, to be close to me, and if sex had to be first then it was better that I was out of it. I am ashamed to say, that I was no way a prim and proper young adult. Partying and sex were a big part of my life.

In my early years away from home when I was single, I knew it was a case of using men. Use them and ditch them. *They deserve it. They're all a useless bunch after one thing with one-track minds.* I never let them hang around to find out if they were decent or not, and I didn't care because I knew none of them were.

I remember eating for comfort and sticking my fingers down my throat 'til I puked it all back up again, or else I'd exercise until I couldn't move anymore. *Eat, but don't get fat.* It became a losing battle. I got fat anyway. I used that when Mom had some health issues. I couldn't figure out why this would be happening, so to cope, I'd eat and then puke.

The very last time I used alcohol to numb myself was when I found out I had possibly been cheated on. My trust level was so high then, and to think that my boyfriend could have cheated and lied was unthinkable. Another time I'd been used, possibly another time I'd live with it. That was, I think, the hardest struggle of trust into the smallest time space I've ever had. *Do I believe him or end it? Am I being used or am I overreacting? Am I imagining it or is it real? Should I be smart and get out now?* Total confusion. *I'll drink.*

I drank 'til I fell asleep. I guess in all reality it's the way I've coped and been conditioned (by myself) to deal. *Go numb. Think about it later.* I've never done it since and hadn't done it for a long time before. Some learned behaviors are hard to break. I found myself focusing the other night and never even realized Gord was talking to me. It was like leaving my body, lying there motionless. My mind a blank. I had no idea where it was. When the terror of the feelings were gone it was safe to come back.

I remember lying awake for hours as a child worrying until daylight. About anything. I'd pretend I was asleep when Dad was in my room and then I'd lay awake most of the night. I don't know how I functioned during the day. Not until about 1985 or '86 did I finally go to bed and was able to go to sleep without worrying. I remember getting up in the middle of the night and checking and rechecking to make sure that anything I had to do, whether it was close a door, put a book out so I'd take it to school, or flush the toilet, it was almost like an obsessive-compulsive behaviour.

I could never talk about my feelings because they always had to do with pain of abuse, hate, anger, helplessness. If I didn't talk about how I felt, my secret would be safe. I still do that even now, even after my secret's been told. I am getting better, though. The words are slowly coming, but sometimes now it's as though I need to keep from talking about it so much so it doesn't overtake Gord's thoughts, his chance to talk, his chance to get away from it all.

What do I do? To go for broke now and get it all out is probably the best; the sooner I do, the sooner this nightmare can be over. More and more now all I see in the back of my mind as I read and write is my father's face. It's like an inset on a television set. A shadow on a wall. I had a prime opportunity to tell my dad how he so drastically screwed up my life. I had gone to tell him I was leaving my second husband. I will never forget what he asked me: "Do you think that the problems you are having now are because of the relationship we had?" I said no and immediately left.

"Relationship," he called it! That rotten...! Downplaying his sick, perverse actions and making it sound like

I was a part of it! I should have told him then what a sick excuse of a person he was. I should have told him then that if it wasn't for him I wouldn't be married to the person I am and that he really should have liked him. But I didn't say it. No, no, instead I passed up the opportunity and let him think that what he'd done was forgotten. If he had asked me when I was half-stable, he would have got it, and that's probably why he chose that time because he knew I could only handle so much at once. The word "relationship" to him obviously means something different than it does to the rest of the world. Totally hopeless approaching him about it. He'd probably make it sound like I liked it in that pigheaded, arms-crossed, eyebrows-up look of his. I can't do it anymore. If I have flashbacks tonight, I don't know what I'll do. I'm just glad he lives a long way away.

I feel like someone totally different writing this. I don't usually have all this hate, let alone write it. I feel like the young girl who lived at home with her parents. Full of hate. Now I remember feeling like this all the time. This is the person coming out that I used to be. It almost feels good, as though I remember who I used to be. I'd forgotten being so full of hate all the time. Maybe this is good, maybe I can keep going back and find out who I was before I was this hateful person. Maybe I can go back far enough to remember and feel like the little girl Janet. I hope I can.

MARCH 8, '93

How Old Was I?

I don't know if it was the first time. Now my gut says it was. He was drunk, there were people sleeping in my room. I was in the back of the truck in our sleeper. He came out there, I was asleep, he was drunk. I was scared. I had to be quiet. I don't know if anyone else was in there or not. I always fell asleep on my stomach because that made it hard to get at me. I wasn't easily accessible that way. I'd pretend I was asleep so I didn't feel guilty. Maybe he would leave me alone then. *Would he come tonight?* Always at night, I think. Abuse me, then he'd give me a hug, tell me he loved me and leave.

Confused. Guilty. *This is scary. I feel scared, shaky. What is Mom doing, will she come? She can't find out.* Dad would tell me, "You know what it would do to your mother if she found out." *Mom is going away again tonight. I'm scared every time she leaves. I hate it, I want to go with her. I know what will happen.* Where is Brad when this happens? I can't remember. My hair is standing on end writing this. *He is finally gone. I can go to sleep now. He won't be back tonight. It's over, I can relax.*

I have to read and turn the light off and pretend to be asleep early in case he comes. I'm on the couch, him and his buddy are drunk. Someone is sleeping in my bed. I'm in the living room. Is his buddy sitting there watching? Dad has his hands on me, I'm not sure where. I'm trying not to move. I can see his buddy's face is showing. What's happening? We are in the basement of someone's house. Dad comes in drunk. He is touching me. I can't move, I can't say anything. *Where is the rest of my family?* I don't know. I lay awake all night.

I used to sleep on the far side of the bed, and he'd move me over. It was always dark, or light was coming in from another room. I never opened my eyes. I didn't want to look at him. I'd lay after he left and sometimes cry myself to sleep. I remember getting aroused sometimes. *Guilt. Shame. Guilt.* I'd only open my eyes and focus if I knew he couldn't see them. No blinking. It was like a stare face. My eyes didn't seem to move even if they were closed or open.

I wonder if it started when Mom was in the hospital all winter? What year was it? It seems Brad was in about grade six. I'd have been in grade four, maybe. Was I that young or was I eleven or twelve years old? In 1972 we had that brown couch. I am back to ten years old... at least then... or eleven. Being at Ressor Lake in 1971...

something stands out in my mind, something bad. Nine years old then. The green truck with the top on it. Brad figures that was 1973. I called him to quiz him, never telling him my purpose. Eleven years old again. My eyes close tight, I'm not sure what I think about when he leaves. My arms are tight beside me. My whole body is tight. To this day, I suffer from tension all over in my body. I'm lying on my stomach still. I don't move until I can relax. Sometimes I fall asleep like that and wake up later. Crickets, I hear crickets. I hear coyotes, I hear the dogs bark. Laddie... we have our dog Laddie.

MARCH 10, '93

Never Let Hurt Show

I'm sorry I don't really know you very well. I've only had a few meetings with you; there are only hits and misses in our relationship. I've seen lots of photos of you from birth to present and I'm not sure how many of those I remember simply because of the photo. I might only remember them because I've seen them so many times. Your grade two picture looks as if you're on top of the world. It looks as if you feel how I do when I'm at my best. I do remember that outfit, green and yellow, that you're wearing. It was my favourite of most of them. That blue winter coat with the flowers on the inside collar.

I think you still felt great then. I remember how you and your little friends would lay awake hours and hours at night laughing, giggling, until you'd get caught. It still never stopped you. I remember how proud you were wearing that red dress with the lace trim. You were still okay then, I think. Somewhere between grade five and grade six, life became difficult... Was it because you were hitting puberty? You got very fat. You looked very unhappy. I remember you spent as much time away from home as you could. I look at your pictures and you seem so grown up, in some of them you look so far away... lost... hurt.

There isn't anything I can do to help you. The only thing you can do is excel in other ways. Use your sense of humour to get by. You are a tomboy, I know that much. The boys always let you play with them when they won't let the other girls. Why is that? It's not because you're old enough to play games like doctor or anything. Maybe it's because you're so tough. I remember you being very tough when you were younger. You never let hurt hurt you. Physical or mental hurt. You never cried or tattled on anyone. Anyone who tattled, you'd sooner tease or pick on. It was a sign of weakness to tell on them.

You were the girl in grade six who could hold a magnifying glass in the sun on your skin till it burned. You were always tough. Anything anyone else could do, so could you, or you could do it better. Remember when you went to a friend's house halloweening? You were still trick or treating and her dad hid your candy on you. Remember thinking he wasn't safe either then? You must have been trick or treating the same time your father was doing terrible things to you. My God, you must have been young then. When did you stop trick or treating? Grade five or grade six?

Back to ten or eleven years old. Was he doing that to you when you were younger, but it never seemed strange? Perhaps it was years before. Will you ever be able to remember to tell me about it? I have a hard time getting to know you. Perhaps Susan can get us together so we can have a closer relationship. I'd love to know you better, but I don't know how. You seem so shallow, so hard to get to know. So protective, you are. It seems you've been like that a long time. Now I'm starting to see where we are very much alike. People tell me that about myself, and now I'm beginning to see just how hard a shell I have around me. Always tough. Never let hurt show.

You must have been going through hell. A little girl having to be so tough. You were scared of your father before you even went to school. Remember the time you smashed your finger in the grader and you didn't cry? There was blood coming through your coat from your hand in your pocket, and you walked right by him. You finally stopped when he hollered at you. Didn't you trust him then? How come you were so afraid of him? Was he mean, violent? Any kid I saw do that now would make me wonder.

Who were you going to tell? Did you think no one would help? Did you think you'd get into trouble? Had you stopped depending on him already then? The tough little girl. Who are you, really? There had to be more to

you than that. How come you don't ever remember putting your arms around your father and feeling safe? It
seems to me you always felt uneasy sitting on anyone's
knee when you were small, even your grandfather's.

I don't know you very well at all, but I do know that
you must have been brave. Who looked after you? Your
brother always has. Your mother used to cover up for
you. What kind of person must your father have been if
your mother always felt she had to calm the storms for
you? Was she afraid of him too? I can't imagine having
to do that now for S, to protect him from his father's
outbursts. I'd never dream of it. If S ever hurts himself,
he runs right to his father, never afraid he'll get into
trouble, never thinking about anything, just being held
and loved. Isn't that the norm? I know it is. How come
you couldn't have lived like that?

Any way I look at it, I wasn't older than eleven or
twelve years old when it started. Or is that when I realized it was bad? How long before... my God.

MARCH 15, '93

Things I Grieve For

I do grieve quite a bit. I never used to until I started therapy; not fully, anyway. Now I can sit or lay and cry. It hurts, but it is a part that has to happen. I know that. I don't have to be alone, either. I have Gord. I can tell him what I grieve for. He tries to understand, he encourages me. He is the only one I've ever told, and I am glad it was him. No one in the whole world could have been better to tell. What do I grieve for?

I grieve for:

- the pain I lived with as a child that suppressed my everyday living
- the things I could have done
- the person I could have been
- Brad, and the mental confusion he had to have as a child to live in the same house
- Brad now still living there, trying to live separately, and his own life
- Mom, who I feel hasn't been truly happy

- Dad, and the pain I see in his eyes sometimes when he looks at me
- the child – myself – who I can't get in touch with
- the loss of many happy memories I've forgotten because they were clouded by the feelings of the abuse filling me
- the anger that for many years ate at me and no doubt resulted in lost opportunities
- my self-esteem that prompted such negative results as the demise of my first marriage, the choice of my second husband, alcohol abuse and meaningless sexual relationships
- lost time spent finding cures for headaches, stomach pain and depression
- the years I spent having to stay busy all the time so I wouldn't think about it
- not getting myself help sooner than this
- most of all, now I grieve for the turmoil this has caused in my new life with Gord
- the unhappiness I see in Gord's eyes when I'm sad
- the time I'm having to spend now to heal when I could be enjoying my life to the fullest

This I know, however, will allow me to live my life to the fullest I possibly can, and I'll just have to accept that God chose me to take this challenge and make it worthwhile.

This process of acknowledging and healing is the biggest, most meaningful challenge in life I've had to face to date. Maybe second only to the surviving the abuse and getting by day to day.

All these things I grieve for, and sometimes it is almost overwhelming.

I grieve for:

- having to avoid my parents for now
- the closeness we shared when I lived there
- not being able to be honest with them right now and maybe ever
- lying to my friends about how great my life is right now

Maybe I'll think of more later.

It hurts terribly to grieve, and it strikes whenever. I never know when it's going to hit, but I try to remember that it's positive and must happen. I just wish I could spare Gord in some way. One positive thing about Gord being with me through this, though, is that I can truly trust one person and their love for me, which I always thought was impossible before. I didn't have the capability or capacity for it. He has broken the wall between trust and me. It's taken over twenty years for anyone to do that. He and I can do anything now. I truly believe that. I thank God for him.

MARCH 15, '93

This is What I Would Say to Him

"Sit down here and listen to me. I have something I want to say. I want you to listen, and please don't interrupt. It's taken a long time for me to finally say something. I know one time you opened the air for this conversation and I avoided it, but now I'm dealing with it and I'd appreciate it greatly if you thought before you responded. I don't want a response now. I want one when you've thoroughly thought about it.

"Remember when you asked if my divorce had anything to do with what happened when I lived at home between us and I said no? Well, it did. I said that then because I wasn't ready to accept what had happened, I wasn't ready to face it or what impact it had on my life. I was too stressed, too weak, too hurt then to face another whole issue. Back then it probably would have meant total devastation of my life. Well, now I'm ready.

"I've been going to therapy, and I've told Gord about it. He's the only one who knows besides Susan, my therapist. Don't panic and don't say anything. Please listen, and please uncross your arms; what I have to say is important. Since I've moved I look at life differently. It's like looking back there and for the first time seeing the whole picture. I never realized before that the sexual abuse had such an impact on my life. I was going to wait until you died, or Mom died, before I dealt with it. Then I realized the longer I waited, the more damaged my life became. It was like I couldn't live life to the fullest possible for me now if I didn't deal with it.

"I can't believe I'm doing this. Just listen, don't say anything and don't get up and leave. I have cried, I have laid awake at night, I have had panic attacks in the middle of the night and the day. I don't even feel anymore sometimes. I have great days, in-between days, very depressed days. All these feelings I'm having are very confusing. I don't even think I want to know why you did it. It's not important for me to hear your side of the story, because it doesn't count. I'd like to think that sometimes you feel bad about it, and whether you know it or not you are totally to blame, not me, not Mom, not Brad, not anyone but you.

"For years I've lived with this secret, this disgusted feeling about myself, because you sexually abused me, and don't look at me with that look. Sit down. I'm mad. You're damned right, I'm mad. I'll make you a list of reasons because right now I'm too angry to tell you all of them. You had no right to do those things to me. I was your daughter, a little girl who was supposed to be protected by her father. Sure, you protected me, or tried to, from other men. That was probably because you didn't want anyone else to touch me the way you did.

"It's supposed to be beautiful, it's supposed to be between two people who love each other. It's something sickening and repulsive for a father to do to his daughter. All my life I paid for that. I don't even remember what it was like to be a little girl. For years I got shit for drinking, partying, digging holes in my hands, and it was all because you did that to me. I couldn't tell anyone. Sure, you clothed me, fed me, gave me almost everything I wanted, yet you took the biggest part of my life away from me. You took my trust, my self-worth, my self-esteem and most of all, you took my childhood. I don't know what it's like to be a child. I can never get that back.

"I'm also worried that you may have done the same to Brad. Be quiet, it's my turn. For years I've watched you control everyone in this house. You could never control me after I left. You know why? Because your opinions and what you have to say about the way I live my life aren't important to me; never have been and never will be. I can only hope that this churchgoing you are so involved in now is for the right reasons. I think sometimes you're looking for forgiveness there. I like to think that the only reason you go is because you feel guilty and are dealing with it. If you aren't, my advice to you is to deal with it now so that when you die you can look back and say "yes, I did that to my daughter. I'm sorry for it. I understand the pain and grief she had to go through for it and I have paid greatly for it myself, but now I'm at peace like she is."

Then I get up to leave and hope he doesn't drink to forget what I've said. The next move is his.

MARCH 16, '93

Feeling Victory

A day off the hard work. Time to think about the good things in my life. Saturday morning, I woke up feeling bad and the phone rang. It was my friend and her husband. Totally unexpected, we spent the day with them. They drove here and then we went into Edmonton. We saw the boat show and then went to the harness races.

Last night I did my homework and called my parents. It was nice to hear them. I do miss them, even though. I had to call to see if how I felt about them was real. I enjoyed talking to them both. It's been a while now since I have.

Gord surprised me tonight with a song: "She Don't Know She's Beautiful." What can I say? He is the dearest person in the whole world. I can't imagine how I'd feel about myself through all of this if he didn't make me so special every day. I'd like to do more for him. I feel like I don't, but maybe when I get most of this behind me my love can shine through more for him as his does for me now. I know I'll have the capacity then to smother him. I can't describe how overwhelming the feeling of his love is sometimes; his towards me and mine toward him. It's almost too good to be true, but I know it is. Despite the healing process I'm having to get through now, I couldn't ask for anyone more loving, gentle, trustworthy, sentimental and handsome, and there is no one else could I love more.

I went to bed last night with a feeling of victory. A feeling that I knew I was going to be on top when this was all over. I know I will and I'll have Gord right there with me. Life is great!!

MARCH 21, '93

I Am a Deserving Person

What triggers the worst feeling of self-worth and sadness more so than just the everyday ones?

I just figured out something. I feel terribly guilty about the time I spend healing and not with Gord. I feel terribly guilty about not making love to him, even though I don't feel up to it right now. He gives so much of himself to me. He waits on me hand and foot. He loves me dearly. That guilty feeling is coming from the little girl in me. Do I feel because he gives so much I should be giving my body to him because he wants it? That's how my father made me feel. He gave me lots, controlled, of course, everything I did, but he figured he could have my body to do with it what he wanted because of it. That's where these guilty feelings come from. They are from then, not now. All my life I've felt like I've owed those close to me for what they chose to do for me.

It's at times like these the tears come, the feelings of self-worthlessness, the deep depression.

I feel like Gord will be mad at me when I say no or avoid lovemaking. My father used to get mad at me if I wouldn't let him touch me. *He won't love me if I don't. I can't live without love.* This is what's going on now, those are the feelings I'm having now. I can relate to them now.

I must tell myself that I own my own body. I don't have to feel guilty for saying no. If anyone wants to be mad because of that, it's their problem, not mine. I don't create their feelings, damnit!

I have to free myself from guilt. I don't owe anyone anything. I can give freely. They too must be able to give freely.

* I am a deserving person. I do not owe for those things I receive. I deserve all the love and affection I get.

* I have every right to say no. I own my own body. I am responsible for my feelings about that and Gord is responsible for his feelings about that. I do not have to feel guilty. I do not have to feel insecure.

Cleaning the house Friday made me feel good. I felt useful, like I had accomplished something. Little things like that help.

Positive Things About Myself
- I am cuddly and affectionate with Gord
- People at work like me and my sense of humour
- My friends are always happy to hear from me
- I feel I look great in my red dress and my black one

- I am good at my job
- I am generally neat and tidy about the house
- I am healthy and in good shape
- Gord thinks I'm beautiful
- I have some true friends
- I am working hard at dealing with my abuse and trying to get through it quickly
- I am accepting a large challenge
- I am not about to quit because it is very hard some days

I will not tune out the loving things Gord tells me about myself. I will think about them from now on and learn to believe them. I do trust him, and therefore the things he says are true.

About this time, my psychologist introduced me to a most helpful and still-to-this-day highly referred book titled *Recovery of Your Inner Child* by Lucia Capacchione PH.D.[*] I highly recommend it to anyone that has experienced childhood trauma of any kind.

Here you will begin to see interactive writings between my adult self and my inner child.

[*] www.luciac.com/recovery-of-your-inner-child/

MARCH 29, '93

That Little Girl

It's okay, Janet, you are safe now. I won't ever let him touch you like that again. I'm older and grown up. I can speak for both of us now. I promise I won't let anyone hurt you like that again.

How come you weren't here then? I'm still back here and I can't get to where you are. You left me behind. Alone. With no one. I've been crying and empty ever since. How could you do that? Look at me.

I'm sorry, Janet. I didn't have any other choice. I had to leave you there. It was the only way I could get away. I'm so sorry I left you now, but I had no other way. I know it's hard for you to understand, but then I didn't know you and I didn't realize I had left you behind. Now I can see that. I can never make it up to you.

I have to go now. I don't like being out when I'm so tired like now. I can't feel like this for long at a time.

Please come back tomorrow if you can. I need someone to be with me.

I will try to find you tomorrow and you can come looking for me in case I can't. I don't want to leave you now, but it's your choice and I understand. Put your arms around yourself and give yourself a big hug. I wish I could take care of you.

I'm going now. I can't stay awake.

After she left:

I can't believe it. It was like getting in touch with the dead. Like an out-of-body experience. The first time she came to me, the first attempt to make contact. She's still reaching out. She's so sad, though. I feel very bad. I wish I could help more. I will. We'll talk lots until we have nothing left unsaid.

I can still feel her presence; perhaps it will always be here now. That would be nice. It feels comforting to be together again. Even though it's painful at the same time. She lives in me. It's hard to believe. That little girl is there!

MARCH 30, '93

I'm Four or Five Now

It seems to me I feel guilty about leaving my child behind. At the same time I was feeling guilty, I was feeling somehow comforted, knowing that I could reach her even if only for a short while. Gord asked me if I could bring her here, but I can't, not yet. It's as if she doesn't trust me enough yet. We have to work at it slowly. She is there, alone and sad, but wants to stay there because she feels safe. She is not feeling safe from him, but she's been there so long she feels security. Only I understand.

Are you here with me, Janet? Don't hide. I want to see you, to talk to you, to help you.

I'm here.

I feel different today after I'd met you last night, like a weight had been lifted from my shoulders. Like a new hope had shone on my life.

How could you think about me like that? I'm not very fun and I'm really just a little girl that has been forgotten about.

I don't know what to say to that. I have indeed forgotten about you.

You ignore me sometimes. Most of the time. You don't play much, try new things, or do fun things much.

I do think I'm more fun now than I was before. I'm becoming more spontaneous and laugh a lot more again. Will you help me splash my feet in the puddles and run from the monsters again?

I do that. I say monster at the bottom of the stairs and run up as fast as I can before it gets me. I'm four or five now. I'm my Daddy's little girl. I'm his pride and joy. I feel like I'm his big girl. I can do anything he wants me to. I'm a tomboy, you know. See my big cat Tommy? I can hardly carry him. I used to have Whitey, my goose, but he disappeared. His soft white feathers would rub my face and his neck would lay on mine. I am always walking with my nose in the air and my chest out when I'm with Dad. Mom just smiles. Her and Brad talk a lot. Brad lets me play with him and his friends lots. Most of the time I think he feels sorry for me if I have no one to play with. He takes good care of me. He goes to school. I watch Mr. Dressup, Chez Elan and Friendly Giant every day. Mom cooks and bakes and Dad works in the field. It's spring now, I think. Everything is neat about spring.

Why is spring your favourite season?

Just is. I always feel proud in spring. I feel like I'm the only little girl in the world. No one else has it like me. I'm happy. I am me and I don't want to be anyone else. I laugh a lot. Lots of fun burying dead mice. I put little crosses on their graves. It's hard to get Laddie to stay away.

I wish I could stay like this forever. I go in the old trailer and play house. I have a pink tea set. It smells like mice and wet wood in there. I play there a lot. I go to Doris and Willy's and play cards. She always giggles when she laughs. I like going there and she always has cookies too. I'm getting tired, but I'd like to stay here because it feels good. I'm happy and I'm proud and the world goes on around me. Will you come back again? Got to go, 'bye.

See you later, little girl.

Amazing. I finally got back there. I finally got through to when I was a little happy girl. It's like shock; it's hard to believe how this works. Am I crazy? No, the memories are too real, the feelings take over when she's writing. I remember that nose-up, chest-out walk I had, like I was everyone, everything.

I remember my missing teeth, the feeling of my tongue on a loose tooth, the hole after it was gone. I remember living in the green house and sitting on the bed, and I think Dad pulled one of Brad's teeth by slamming the door with a string tied to it. I remember that happening once in the new house too, I think. I remember the metal bathtub in the green house and I think there was a portable toilet in there for nighttime. A green curtain, maybe. Was it on the window?

I used to spend hours in that old trailer playing house. There was an old grey pullout table in there. I remember getting my finger stuck in it one day when I was putting the side up. It made my stomach sick. It hurt, and I think I got a blood blister. There used to be an old couch in there too. I remember building mud pies, and the smell of them. I made them out behind the new house too, under Mom and Dad's bedroom windows. Brad had a yellow and black Tonka with the back loader and front bucket. I saw one at the flea market the other day.

I got back; I broke through the wall. I can't believe it. I always thought before that the things I remembered were from pictures. There are no pictures of these things. They were real. I remember. I've found her!

I think if I can keep talking to her she will tell me everything I need to know. And hopefully I can help her out so she can live with me. She can be happy again and live here.

APRIL 21, '93

My Moods, I Can't Control Them

Three weeks since I've last worked here. My last session with Susan was too much, I think. We went through my photo album, and she told me how old I looked as a child. I was living the life of a married, unhappy woman as a child. I was ready to kill when I came from my session. Then I went to watch Gord curl and spent the time doing other things. I never dealt with it when I should have. The anger is there, so close. I've managed to keep it hidden long enough not to go nuts. It's getting me bad, though.

Sex has been a problem ever since. Gord and I went to Canmore and rented a small cabin for Easter weekend. We had fun together. We always do, though. But it wasn't free. We were very close and needed that holiday together, but I was fighting the little girl in me. My moods are changing rapidly again. I can't control them. Dizziness, sadness, uncontrollable laughter— I never know what will be next. I've been avoiding discussing the whole issue and it seems to build a wall between us, for me, anyway. I seem to lose total contact with the people who are important to me. The overwhelming closeness becomes far away at times. I hate it. Today I thought seriously about getting drunk somewhere. I can't seem to find a proper place, a way to vent it all. I'm scared. I don't know what to do next.

I feel guilty because I don't want to make love. I feel guilty because Gord is very sad today. I feel guilty because I know his moods are a reflection of mine. I feel like I'm letting him down. I feel guilty because I haven't worked in so long. I feel guilty because I don't want to see Mom and Dad. I feel, in a way, like everything has changed so much, so fast, and I can't keep up.

Are you there Janet, little Janet? There are so many things I need you to help me with. Can you tell me where your mother was? How can I help you? How can we compromise on sex? Gord and I had such a beautiful sexual relationship, but now it seems to struggle. I have a hard time. The desire is almost impossible to find at times, yet his is so sexy, so masculine, so gentle, so loving. I need that. Tell me what you need and maybe we can compromise.

Here I am. I've been close to you lately. The puppy you found in Banff was for me. When you pick him up *it's me who hugs him and talks to him. I played with the little bird and with No Name. It was me riding the pallet jack at work the other day, laughing and screaming. Didn't I sound like a little girl? It was me who got out of bed this morning with tears in my eyes. It was me who didn't want to be around anyone this morning. I'm with you at work all day. I'm the one who laughs at the little things. I'm the one your work buddy called a giggle puss, and you're the one he calls the softie.*

I guess you're right. I do laugh and stuff a lot lately. More than I used to. It's you who needs to be hugged and held so much by Gord. It's you who doesn't want to make love... you're afraid to, aren't you?

To me it doesn't mean love. It means hurt. I'm afraid he'll leave me. He's the only one I've ever known. He takes care of me. He'll do anything for me. I love him so much. He is all I have. He is all I want.

SOMETIME APRIL/MAY '93

Things That Make Me Feel Better

- Being able to say no and not feeling guilty or insecure
- Pampering myself by having a nice relaxing bath, doing my nails, shaving my legs, deep conditioning my hair etc.
- Pampering Gord when he least expects it or when he needs it
- Giving S a hug just because
- Having the house look neat and clean with the sun shining in every room
- Writing letters to my friends letting them know that they are important to me and thought of often
- Going for a walk in nice weather and seeing all the beautiful things there are to see
- Listening to music and visualizing how happy Gord and I can be and all the fun we can have together

MAY 8, '93

I Will Protect You

Please don't let me live in anger and disruption anymore. I need to be able to control my life. Others can't bring their chaos into our home. I'm just getting so I can come out, be free and not worry about anyone interfering. I need more attention than you've been giving me. I am happy you took all our stuff from the farm. It's about time you did that. Learn to take better care of me. You're all I've got right now. Gord is busy with his own children. You have to look after me. You told me you would. That's his responsibility, and I'm yours. You know it will always be just us. You and me. You can't trust anyone else you know. I know that.

Janet, we trust Gord, he loves us both and there is room for us in his heart too. What did he do? I thought you liked him and we could trust him? Please tell me if something has happened to change that.

He didn't come with me today. I needed him. He knew I did. But he wouldn't today.

He offered to, Janet. It was you who didn't say anything. He said he would. You have to learn to speak out.

I thought I did. You just look after me now.

Are you jealous, Janet, that there are two children here that need to be looked after?

No, I'm not jealous. It's just that every time I need you now there isn't time. All you guys talk about is legal stuff. I thought when we came here everything would be different. We left your parents' house, we told about the abuse but no, that isn't enough, now there's this thing. I've had all I can stand. I just want to be happy for a change.

Janet, before we couldn't control the abuse or control our own lives. This we can control. There is a date set up for next week to decide legalities. It will take a bit, but Gord will look after this. I must help him, but believe me, it won't be like this for long. I promise you we will not live like this forever. We do have control over it and you will be protected. I will protect you. I'll stand up for you. You'll never have to live like that again, not like before, and not like now. We'll get through this. You just trust me, Janet—we will, one way or another.

MAY 13, '93

No Children

You're upset tonight, aren't you, Janet?

I am a bit yes. It's been like it used to be the last two days. Everyone was happy. Now tonight Gord is upset because of a message left on the machine. So what? He doesn't have to do anything about it.

I think he's upset because it brings to light the fact that he may have deal with chaos again.

Is it the chaos or is it the child that makes him upset? You better think about that, Janet.

You're just saying that because you felt nobody, meaning your Dad, wanted you when you were a child. I don't think it's fair that you can judge everyone by that! Some people really do love their children just because.

Do they? You've never had them. Why?

Ouch. You are where my fight comes from. There was no way I wanted to bring kids into this world to have them grow up the way I did. And frankly, I could and can hardly deal with myself. Why would I bring someone into the world that I wasn't wanting to be responsible for? I have seen too many times when women and men have children for the wrong reasons. It was my choice and remains my choice for many reasons.

MAY 18, '93

No Control, No Feeling

I feel nothing for anyone. I am alone again. I must look after myself. Gord says to stop feeling sorry for yourself. I don't care. Nothing he says can hurt me. I am so solid. I am hard. I cried earlier, but it's so stupid. I drank beer, and I would like another one. I can't even sit back. This is a familiar feeling. No control. No feeling. I am rocking. I have gone back now, further than I ever have. I feel like I'm in big trouble. Who will care for me now? No one. He has worries of his own. It's just me again. Are things so different here? I don't have a say in anything. Stuck in the middle. I need to get help. Where do I go now? I don't care. I'll go to work tomorrow. Everything is okay there as long as I do my job. I don't have to be anything or anyone there. I'm just Janet. Funny me.

AUG. '93

Ugly, Dirty, Not Loved

It's been a long time since I've written. I do regret that. A lot has happened since. The bad dreams are less frequent now, and depression is less frequent. We've moved into our new home. I've been neglecting you, my little Janet. Gord has discussed it with me many times. How come I never work anymore? Have I given up? I've been busy trying to work on my sexuality and I know now that I need to spend equal time with my inner child. My weight is up and down, my moods are the same. There is little talk in our house anymore of the abuse until it comes to sex and my dreams. Maybe I am trying to forget. When I see my parents, it takes days to recover afterward. I am feeling very ugly lately; not attractive at all. I can hardly stand to look at myself in the mirror. Gord keeps telling me I'm beautiful and attractive but I don't see myself as that. Talk to me, Janet.

I've always felt ugly, dirty, not loved. I always ate when I was unhappy. I'm very sad now. I feel bad

because I'm here and I'm safe and I'm finally okay
without them. I miss my brother. He needs help and
I can't do it for him. I feel bad for my mother because
she is blind and will not see. For my father I feel dis-
gust and sometimes sorry for him, but most of all I feel
for Brad. He has not learned yet to face it and he's
doing everything to hide. I have to tell him I'm getting
help. I need more help. I want to see Susan.

AUG. 22, '93

Getting Worse

Bad days lately. I'm depressed, big time. Work is hectic. I can't get enough sleep or enough relaxation; I can't relax, period. Gord has been snappy at me lately, I guess because I've been the same. He doesn't understand. If I was physically sick or hurt I wouldn't be expected to carry on as usual. Miss bubbly, Miss responsible, Miss congeniality. But because nothing is seen on the outside it's everything as usual. I can't do it anymore. I haven't eaten in two days... anything I eat comes back. It's getting worse now instead of better. Tuesday I see Susan again. I feel like I don't want to get up in the morning. Why?

I feel bad for Gord. One of these days he's going to say he's had enough. We spent a week out on Pigeon Lake, just the two of us. It was great. I think I need a month or two of that. No noise, no obligation, no work, just nothingness. Maybe a longer period of time would allow me to relax and put things into perspective before it was time to start back.

I really messed up big time today. I think I'll try to eat and go to bed.

AUG. 25, '93

Sacrificing My Life to Save Theirs

We went to Susan yesterday. I went in first. The bottom line, between what the two of us could figure out, is this: I've come a long way in a short time. She told us both again that she's never seen anyone move this fast. I've been in eight times since February and I'm at this point already. She says the quickest she's seen to date is once-a-week or twice-a-week appointments every week for six months to get to where I am, and those are the best.

I guess I should be proud of myself. She says intellect has a lot to do with it. I can blow my own horn a little bit. Here I am on this road, and my depression and periods of waking unconsciousness are expected at this time. I can now choose to forget it and go on living the way I have, and it may get better, but chances are not much. Or I can confront him with it and let him make the choice as to whether he wants to have no relationship with his daughter at all or have the best as can be expected.

I can't go on playing the avoidance game and have it looming in the back of my mind. If I forget the whole thing, I would be defeating my purpose of facing it in the first place. What would I have accomplished? I've always known what happened. Maybe I haven't remembered it as vividly as since February, but it would then become finished business instead of half finished. I could run the risk of losing my parents completely. I don't know that it's what I want. I don't think that it is, and I don't know that it would happen. That's the risk, that's what I have to deal with now. I said to Susan, "Just because I've had to live through it again, does everyone have to suffer now?"

She thinks if I don't I'll be sacrificing the rest of my life to save theirs. I'm young and healthy with great potential for extreme happiness.

Maybe he knows, maybe he is waiting for it to happen, maybe he is prepared. Maybe he thinks I wouldn't dare. Who knows? Yesterday I was so angry, and today I'm too tired, too exhausted, too beat to even be angry. My mood swings are atrocious. Maybe I'm okay today in that aspect because subconsciously my mind is made up. I am preparing myself. As Susan said, as an adult intellect I know it was wrong; does my little girl know it was wrong, or is she still feeling guilty? You were here yesterday, Jani, are you today? We have to talk about this. I need to know how you feel.

You told me you'd look after me. You said Gord would too. Who will take care of me if he doesn't? Can you? I could always go to Mom and Dad if I had a problem out of the family. What if I can't anymore? I think Dad is waiting for me to say something. He did call once when Mom wasn't there. He does it a lot. Maybe I should say it then. I have to say it sometime, but I don't want to not have parents. Surely, he would love me enough, in a good way, to want me to be family still. Maybe he'd be happier if it was out in the open. I need to be free. I know it may hurt you and it's hard to do, Janet, but I'm trapped here until it's said. I'm in a cave. I can't be good. I'd like to be, but I'm only a hurt child. Don't expect too much from me. You know what it's like to live with something or someone you can't be happy with and it's going nowhere. You're miserable and so am I. That's me now. I want to be happy and grow up. I want you to be happy, but if I'm not, you're not. If Dad doesn't want anything to do with us he's even less of a dad than I thought, and we don't need him anyway. If he does, maybe we can all go on. If not, at least you and me can. We've done it before all by ourselves, and it's something we didn't do so good, but we're here. You have Gord now too. Maybe someday I'll trust him like you do, but for now it's hard.

I'd like to do it now, Janet, but I have to think it through some more. Thank you for being here to talk to me. I need you now as much as you need me, or even more. It's you who suffered and it's us who live with it. Together we'll get through this, somehow, someway. I'm not going to ask you to be patient because I don't think I want you to, but if you decide you want to be, let me know. We have to work together, now more than ever, because a decision has to made and it has to be right for both of us.

It will ultimately change our lives forever, no matter what we decide. I'll take care of you though, don't worry. You're pretty smart for a little kid, and I feel closer to you now than I ever have.

AUG. 31, '93

Tired of the Crap

Why do I all of a sudden feel such rage? I plan my life with care. I'm sick of it. I'm tired of the crap. I'm tired of crap at work, I'm tired of the crap with the legalities, and I'm even more tired of the crap of this whole sexual abuse garbage!

I've had it!!

The first day I've felt human in weeks and I get screwed around. Others lack of plans are obviously more important than mine STILL!

Maybe I'm fooling myself.

I need to get out and walk.

Unreasonable, Irrational and Unreliable

I've been off work for two-and-a-half days now. This depression has taken over and I'm fighting it all I can. I've never taken off work before, but I just can't stand to be around anyone now. My anger pops out everywhere.

I'm totally unreasonable, irrational and unreliable. Gord is surprised I haven't been like this all along. How I thought it would be over by now. Seven months I've been dealing. I just get over one hurdle and another comes up. My eating and sleeping habits are totally screwed. My sense of humour has moved out, my compassion for others has dwindled. I got up this morning and cleaned house for three hours; it takes my mind off what I feel I have to do. How do I do it? I looked back just now and on March 15th I wrote a dialogue to my father. It's good. I'll use it when the time comes, either in words or in a letter.

Last night Gord and I discussed telling his parents. It's obvious to him too that I've been avoiding them. His mother can see right through me, and she knows something isn't right. I feel by not telling her I could be missing out on one of the great friendships in life. She won't ask, though. I wish she would. Gord said he would tell them if I was there because sooner or later I'm going to have to face them. I'm afraid they'll think I'm not right for Gord and the kids anymore. I'm afraid I shouldn't tell them before I tell my father.

Is it fair? Maybe not, but it also isn't fair that I should miss out more of life because of what he chose to do to me. All of these things are more than I can handle. I'm not drinking or abusing substances, though, and I am very proud of myself for that. I should be a hero one day, but I won't be. There are many other women out there suffering the same things I am. I guess we're what they call the unsung heroes. Will it end with a confrontation of some kind? Will I feel free? I think I will.

OCT. 21, '93

I Have a Goal

My first night at group. A lot of emotions running through me now. A flood. I feel good, though. I feel comfortable, I feel cozy, I feel safe, I feel supported. I feel like I can go through a lot there sharing. Today Gord came and picked me up for lunch. We drove by a backhoe skimming surface pavement off the road and dumping it into a truck. I made mention that there must be a quicker way to do that—it would take forever, or at least a long time. That's what I feel tonight; like a shovel has scraped off some of the hard surface and dug around bottom a bit, lifted out some emotions that were hidden down there. Trapped. They're out now, dancing around free. This is what I want all the time.

I told Gord about it tonight. I said I'd like to know how to be able to keep that hard surface soft all the time. He said, "Put it in a dump truck and take it away." It's funny how things like that happen all in a day. I came home full of feelings, emotions, all mixed. I wanted to bask in the softness of my surface. It took a bit to get relaxed and be able to have those emotions, but when I did all the feelings came back, tears came to my eyes and I cried. They were tears of joy. I had to explain to Gord that I was happy, not sad or hurt.

This is how I want to feel all the time.

Feeling, period. That's what I am. I had to write this down. I had to record this, so I can look back in the days to come and know that I can feel. I know that my goal for group is to make feeling and feeling emotions a habit. I don't want to feel on the surface and just function. I don't want to tune out or space out. I want to be HERE all the time and I want to experience everything and everyone around me. That is my GOAL!!

OCT. 28, '93

Talk of Suicide

Because I can't keep up with my thoughts when I'm driving home from group therapy, I got a voice-activated recorder, so I can drive and collect my thoughts at the same time. These are the transcripts from those recordings.

One of the ladies said something tonight about the offenders' control and how they use it. She then told the story about her brother who said that if she reported the abuse he would commit suicide, which was another form of control that he used on her, and she said tonight that if he did kill himself she would feel guilty for the rest of her life. And that raised a question for me. Is that the reason I don't want to tell other people about it? The only reason I don't want to tell some people about it is because I'm protecting him. I'm protecting Dad, and I don't understand why I'm protecting him. He was there for me at times when I needed him. He fed me, clothed me, gave me a home to live in and worked hard to "otherwise" take care of his family. I asked our group leader the question tonight: why am I trying to protect him? She says it's not the adult me that has the need to confront him or say anything to him, it's the child inside of me. The adult point of view is yes, he was there at other times in my life when I needed him, but it's my inner child that says he abused me, and it was my inner child that suffered.

It's not the adult that suffers; the adult suffers the results of, but it's the child that suffers the abuse. I asked a question that didn't get answered tonight because there wasn't time. And maybe it's something I should ask Susan. How do I confront him as an adult when it's possibly the child that needs to hear what he has to say? It isn't the adult that needs to hear that—it's the child, and I don't know how to relate the two. Do I go to him and say, "This isn't Janet the adult that has this to say, this is Janet the child that has this to say?"

I could feel comfortable doing that. I guess whether he understands or not isn't important. There is no way he could ever understand, unless of course he was abused as a child as well. Then he'd have to do an equal amount of work or more than I have done to get to the point he could ever understand. But I don't think he was sexually abused. I don't know if offenders are or not.

There are people I would like to tell, like Gord's parents, for instance. I'm not allowing anyone into my life right now. Everything remains the same with anyone that knew me before. It's the same old Janet. I can play that game, but I realize that's why I haven't made any friends here now. I feel like I'm the one that's losing again. I'm not losing because eventually it may come, but at the same time, for the time being, I'm not losing, it's more like I'm missing out. I feel I'm missing out. I have no idea what others reactions would be, none whatsoever. It is a fear of getting too close to someone or letting them get close enough to realize there is something wrong because I don't want to tell anyone. In some instances, I suppose with new people I could get close, but it's hard to get close when you're trying to hide a big secret like that. There are so many other things attached to it that I don't speak about because I'm scared all of it will come out. It's the same as it's always been. *Don't communicate, don't get hurt, don't get too close.* Somebody is going to know there is something not right about you, Janet.

One of the people in group mentioned she had told a few people but was met with nothing but disappointment. Their reactions weren't what she expected or needed perhaps.

Half the people in that group have quit their jobs because they can't handle it. I wonder if it's because they can't handle it or if it's because they have more feeling? Do they feel deeper than I do? I wonder about that. I guess everyone handles things differently. They can't seem to function at a regular job and everyday life and deal with what they are dealing with now. I seem to be able to do that, and maybe I'm just fortunate. I don't know.

I do know that I'm very lucky to have all the support I have with Gord because I hear others talk and it sounds like some are very much on their own. It doesn't sound like one has any support system around her other than counseling and the group she's in. I don't know if I could do that. I could, and I would, but thankfully this group exists. I recall feeling like on more than one occasion like if I could just go to sleep and not wake up, or if I just steered the car into that river or over that guardrail, it would all end. It's been quite a while, but I certainly remember feeling like that and I know what I felt like inside all the time—then too. It was a terrible, lonely, empty feeling.

I can't say how much I appreciate Gord. I get everything in my life that I need from him, everything that I never got from anybody else. We have fun together, he takes care of me, he confides in me, I confide in him, and I can trust him one hundred percent with anything and everything. It seems I have everything I want... then why am I so sad all the time?

I have to remember to go and get that book on Saturday when we're in the city at Greenwood's bookstore.

I never knew before tonight was a body memory was. I had never even heard the expression used before. I know I have them. Two of us in that whole group of eight people were very rebellious and promiscuous. Anywhere there was a place to cause trouble you did it, no matter how you could do it, you did it. She explained it to a T.

Whenever you get a large group of people like that together, even a small group, there are some talkers and some that just sit and listen. You know, I always used to be a listener but, damn it, I'm there to get something out of it. And I guess I'm one of the talkers in the group. I have nothing to hide there. Some of those people just kind of sit back and don't say much about anything or give much input or share or anything like that. Me, I'm not quite as introverted as I thought. I guess I'm more introverted with people I know than with people I don't. With people I don't know I can tell just about anything to, but people I love have to fish it out of me. It's the trust thing, I guess. Obviously, there is no other answer to it.

I don't trust. I don't trust people that are close to me. When you get used in a big way like that, it's hard. I don't care who you are. Try to explain that, though. I know what I'm thinking, but I can't explain it to anyone. I guess I have to stop thinking like an adult and start thinking like a child. It's the child I have to heal, not so much the adult. The adult healing will come with the child healing so maybe what I should do to make things easier is to think of everything from my inner child's point of view and say accept Janet as she is now. Janet is too rational, too logical, too responsible. If I can heal a child, I can heal her. So maybe what I have to do when I'm thinking of the confrontation or saying something to Dad or telling him about it is forget about the Janet and think about who Gord calls me sometimes: Jani.

Heal her, please her, she's the one that was hurt. Maybe the rest will all fall into place. Real easy to say, but I don't know how I'll do it. But think about that, Janet. Don't consider Janet, think about what Jani needs. She needs to be set free. Janet has everything she wants. Gord is right; Janet does have everything she wants. It's Jani that doesn't have everything she wants, and she may never get it, but she can be set free if she lets herself. And it's Janet's responsibility to make sure that gets done. I have to nurture my inner child and I have to take care of her, and if that's what she needs then that's what you have to do, Janet. Don't do it for Janet, do it for Jani.

Think of it as if you were talking to someone about their own child. You're not much of a mother and you never will be but you have some very good ideas about how kids should be raised and how they should be taught. Now, if someone was sitting there telling me that their child had been abused, what would you tell them, Janet?

I'd tell them to be open. I'd tell them not to protect the offender. I'd tell them to get all the help that they needed so they could grow up and lead a healthy and happy life. I'd tell them to make sure that whatever that child needed, they got. That's what I'd tell them. Why can't I tell myself that?

No wonder I never have time to pay attention to what goes on around me. I almost think faster than I can talk.

The loneliness I felt when I left the session tonight is starting to leave me and I can't believe it, but I actually shed tears tonight. That's the first time in a long time and that's what I need. It's starting to fade a little bit, though. The numbness is starting to go away.

NOV. 4, '93 (RECORDING)

Shame, Guilt, Lies, Deceit and Secrets

I don't know how I feel. I almost feel like I'm pissed off. I don't know why. Group tonight wasn't exactly how I thought it would be. We discussed shame and guilt and things that we felt guilty about and how guilt worked in our families, but no one was really taught how to deal with it. Maybe they are just trying to make us aware that the only way you can feel guilty is by feeling guilty yourself. And I know nobody can make you feel guilty—it's you that makes yourself feel guilty and maybe that's why I was pissed off tonight; because I already know that and there are lots of people in the room that didn't know that and it's like a great revelation to them. That's something I've known for a long time.

I have taken my control back. I just kind of realized it today. I know that Mom and Dad are coming next weekend. I talked to them on the phone, but I don't feel like before where the anxiety and depression would set in for a couple of days at a time. The reason I'm sure is that the control that was placed on me as an abused child and the guilt I feel was laid on through the years I have control over now. I have taken control, I have taken the reins, and a good indication of that to myself and the reason I have been able to come to that conclusion is the fact that I'm doing this therapy, and I'm working at recovering. It's like it doesn't matter anymore what they do or say. I have a strong enough handle on it, and I have the strength now to kind of let it slide off my back and I don't let them get to me.

When you are being abused as a child and are told, "Don't tell your mother" and "Do you know what that would do to her?" you have a tendency to put up with a lot, to do what it takes to keep the family together, to protect your mom at all cost. And then it becomes one-sided, controlling, and you become easily manipulated. That's how I feel. Easily manipulated into making things happen so that other people, not me, are okay. I'm sick and tired of it. I have done so many things to get my brother out of a bind because my mom would ask me to. If I said no, I would feel bad, but resent being asked in the first place. I always felt manipulated into it. I was doing it because she would feel bad if I didn't. When I moved away, I felt guilt about that. When I don't call and don't know when I'm going back to visit, I feel guilty about that. It's not my responsibility, yet because of the lies, the deceit and the secrets, I feel manipulated and controlled. I guess too there is a part of me that hopes that when this is all said and done, whether I confront my father with this or not, that somehow some of the damages that were done can be repaired and we can still be a family and maybe find some medium of understanding so that we can remain a family and not totally break apart. I know now, and I have been trying to stay emotionally apart from them as much as I can, but I don't want to lose that totally. If anything, I'd like it to be even closer than it has been since I moved away, and the only reason it hasn't been is because I've been dealing with this now and I'm having a hard time being attached to them in any way while dealing with it at the same time. I can't do both. But I hope when this is over I can do both. We can be a family, a close family again, even if we can't see each other as often or more than we do now.

I remember last week when I left I was thinking about how some people in the group don't share. Some people share more and others don't really share at all. One came forward tonight and disclosed her offender, and I realize now that the reason people don't is that, for one, it may be too painful to speak out loud. Another reason is that some people don't share at all and so rather than be contributors to the group, they are takers, and then it becomes about trust again. This lady said she thought it was unfair that she is going there to share and to learn from other people and some people just don't seem to be sharing very much of what's going on inside of them. It's difficult to relate and get anything from them. There is a lot to be said for that. You might learn that your feelings aren't out of the norm for this situation, or that a lot of the things you're going through are the same things they are going through as well. Part of the shame and guilt that some of the other group members were sharing tonight I have been through already. And I feel quite fortunate about that, actually. I guess it's just another indication that perhaps I'm a fast healer. I'm proud of the fact that I am and I'm also proud of the fact that I've been working darn hard to do it.

There is another positive thing I said about myself today. Tonight's group was kind of discouraging. I know I said that, but it's like tonight I've had enough of this crap. I just want to quit. That's what I feel like; almost like I don't want to go back. I'm just not hyped at all tonight. Some of the things that were shared were so heavy.

Someone said they felt guilty because they were abused a few times and by a very early age they started collecting money for it and then when they got older they went out on the streets and sold sex for a short time and now they feel dirty and bad. Somebody else said they always avoid the question of "do you have a boyfriend" or "are you going out with someone" because they don't have any kind of relationship with anyone, nor do they care to. They are not ready for it, and have never had one. Another said sex is scary for them, uncomfortable for them, so they avoid anything that might lead to it.

I can't remember what the others were. I never really realized it, but I guess guilt is an issue for me because I phoned Gord and told him I was going for coffee with some of the girls from group tonight and I heard the disappointment in his voice that I wasn't coming home right away, and I felt guilty about that. That's not a big deal, or it shouldn't be. And now that I think about it, I was chipper and giggly when I talked to him on the phone, but when I heard that in his voice it kind of set me into a different mood. I'm not exactly sure why. It's like I don't want to feel guilty about it and I shouldn't have to feel guilty about it. I know he's there waiting for me and stuff, but, like, this is my thing and I have to be able to do some things for myself and on my own without feeling guilty. And I'm not going to feel guilty about it. I'm just not. This is a start. He may be disappointed, and perhaps if I were him I'd be disappointed too, but I'm not going to feel guilty about it. So there!

I feel mad. I feel pissed off. Again. Why do I feel like that? I just wish this whole thing was over. I'm sick and tired of it. Just forget about it. I have nine more weeks, nine more weeks and then maybe…. It will be the end of another stage, I guess. Like, are there any normal people in this world, or are we all just screwed right up? Is anybody really happy?

NOV. 11, '93 (RECORDING)

Everyone Has a Choice

I seem to be feeling a lot tonight. I'm feeling with my body and not just thinking in my head. That's a good thing. I stayed centered there tonight and I stayed with the program, I guess, if that's what you want to call it. It feels good. We talked about grieving and stuff and I realized also that I somehow associated grieving with weakness. Why now, when I'm thirty-one years old, am I just realizing that grieving isn't a sign of weakness? Maybe it's the choice of words they used tonight: "honor grieving." Take the time to honor grieving, take the time to grieve and realize that grieving is to be honored.

It's like a big light has been turned on. All of a sudden, I realized grieving isn't a sign of weakness, it's part of living. I've always felt that when I was grieving it was something to be embarrassed by or something that strong people didn't do or didn't need to do. I realize that I've always tried to be tough and pretend that things didn't bother me. *Be strong, Janet*, that's always what I think. But there is nothing embarrassing about grieving, and there shouldn't be anything embarrassing about grieving. I realize now that maybe part of me I lost, that part of me that could feel for other people and be warmer to other people and try and take care of other people, or that it didn't even exist for the simple fact that I'm not in touch with my own feelings. If I can't grieve for myself and have to be strong for myself, how can I be sensitive to other people's feelings about things?

At one time in my life I was, and I could. I felt like I could reach out and be there for other people when they needed me, and I just felt closer to other people and not so dissociated from them. I think that's why— because I've lost that somewhere, somehow. So my work now is that I have to figure out a way or set some time aside to be in a safe place that feels good where I can honor my grief for the losses in my life, even the small ones.

Another thing I realized tonight is that I've done a lot of work on grieving after I told Gord about the sexual abuse; however, I haven't spent a whole lot of time grieving over the other losses in my life, and one of those that popped right into my head, first thing, when they said "losses in your life," Janet, was John. I know I spent three days... three days in the apartment with the curtains closed crying and sleeping and puking, and at the same time I was doing that I was taking Valium so I could ease the pain, and after that third day what did I do? I went and drank. I got drunk and I never thought about it. My brain and body did, though. I had nightmares about it, but I never consciously thought about what the loss of John meant to me and how guilty I felt about it and how guilty I still feel about it. I guess I was just so lost in being drunk and partying that I could forget about it. I never spent the time to grieve the loss of my very close friend.

A group member was talking tonight about how she never ever got the nurturing from her parents or her ex-husband she felt she needed, and she mentioned just the holding and the "it's okay to cry and to be held and loved and cuddled." The first thing I thought was that when I was growing up it wasn't that cool to cry about something either, and I don't ever really remember, although maybe it happened, being held when I was crying or anything like that. I'm sure it had to have happened. It's probably because when I needed it most, when I was being abused, I couldn't tell anyone about it.

That's exactly what I get from Gord now, and it feels so good. He's always telling me about how I try and act so tough sometimes and so strong and he holds me and tells me to cry and he honors my grief and I don't even do it.

Sometimes I wonder where he comes from. He has had life's disappointments and hardships and challenges too, but he is so much smarter when it comes to taking care of me than I am. I just sometimes don't think he's real. It feels so good to feel, even though it feels bad—it feels so good. Sometimes I go for such long periods of time without feeling. It just kicked right in tonight. Full bore, heart, head, body everything... it feels!

There are some other things I want to work on. Lately I've been checking in with myself, I guess, especially during intimacy of any kind. I double check that I'm conscious and there and feeling, and that I'm able to feel connected to everything that's going on. I need to remind myself to do that more, especially in the morning, because a lot of times I have no feelings in the morning and during the day at work I notice I am unconscious or not conscious of other people's feelings and what they are telling me. And also, I need to check my consciousness at night, in the evenings when I'm at home with my family and when I'm out with other people. So basically, I need to check my consciousness all the time, is what it boils down to. It's kind of like pinching yourself to make sure that you're there, except it's checking in with your mind to make sure that you are present.

I need to do that more and if I can get in the habit of it, then I think I can become closer to people and not avoid them so much or think I have to. I don't exactly know what I'm trying to say. I think it's that if I can do that, I can become more in touch with everything that goes on around me and therefore enjoy it more rather than sometimes thinking life is a chore and socializing with people is a chore and things like that. I think if I can stay present, I'll have a lot more feelings from my body and not just thinking from my head. I just really need to do that. I need to feel more connected. Some days I feel so dissociated with everyone around me that I feel like I'm just a minute person in the world, and I am, but I have to start feeling more a part of my family and my co-workers, and even part of curling Friday nights. I feel like an outsider. Sometimes I don't feel like I belong there, and it's because I don't allow myself to feel connected to very many things or very many people. If I could start to feel more, be more consciously with it...I can do that. That's my goal; that's what I have got to work for hard now—hard, hard.

We were asked to write a letter to our mothers tonight about what we'd like to say to them. In my letter, I said that I really wanted my mother to get her own life so that she could be as happy as she could be and filled with joy. And that we can take care of ourselves, should be taking care of ourselves, and that her job was to be a mom and not enable other people. Take care of herself and let others be responsible for their own outcomes. We got talking tonight about how everyone is responsible for their own lives and all of us have choices. Those of us in the group have all made the choice that we want a better life and that's why we're there and everyone in this world has a choice to make their life better. All we can do is look after ourselves, and maybe when the time comes that we feel better about ourselves we can help other people make those choices. But everyone is ultimately responsible for their own happiness, and I was doing quite well with it until we started talking about anger. When someone brought up the topic of throwing plates to break them, in that instant I realized all the anger that was built up in me.

I had slammed drawers, doors and everything else my hands could touch over the years. It's always been easier for me to get angry than to cry. The truth is that I always thought of crying as weakness too, and my brother and I grew up seeing anger a lot. My dad would explode, swear, rant. And because I swore never to let him see me cry, anger became my go-to. Breaking something in a controlled way is a plan I'll have to think about and see if I can make happen. Maybe Gord will want to share in it with me. His anger over this whole thing rages inside of him at times. I know it, yet he tries not to let me see it. It would do us both good. We do everything else together and we enjoy being together and I think it would be good.

I think of it as an anger ritual, almost, a celebration in getting some of this anger out. Until today, until that person mentioned it, it was okay. Then all the anger came back to me. The anger towards my mother, the anger towards my father, the anger towards all the things that have kept me from living the life I want to.

And the anger that comes most to the forefront is the anger over all the suffering that Gord and I have had to do because of this. There has been very valuable time lost when we should have been happy instead of dealing with this abuse thing and living like it never happened because it shouldn't have happened! I'd like to share a rage-throwing fest with him, but he isn't as animated as I am, so maybe not. I just want to share everything with him!

NOV. 13, '93 (RECORDING)

I Know I Can Do It

I've had better days this week than I've had in ten months, and it's great because I know I can do it now. I'm getting to see a little piece of the consistently better days that I want now. I'm getting small doses of it at a time and they seem to be getting closer together now. That's what I'm striving so hard to get. Sometimes when you don't have them for a long period of time or you have ones like you've never had before, you don't feel like you can ever be like that, but I know I can be because I had three days like that this week! And I know I can do it.

One day I'm going to listen back on these tapes and I'm going to say, "I can't believe, Janet, that you've come this far." It's all going to seem like a nightmare behind me. It's a struggle, a real struggle, and hard work. But it's something that I need to do and I'm going to be thankful that I've worked this hard one day. I know one day I am.

Until that anger is released it's hard to go on with other things, and I know I've still been moving forward. I have expressed anger on paper and stuff but there is still a lot left in me and that's what I need to do. I think that's what Gord needs to do too; we need to get rid of some of this anger, so we can calm down and not direct it toward each other anymore. If we share it, then we'll have something to laugh about... something to cry about. There will be a common experience for both of us to deal with this whole thing. That's something we don't have very often.

Last night was one of the most beautiful nights I've ever spent with Gord. Our anniversary night was another one of our most beautiful nights. I never lost myself once and it felt so nice. I was there, and I felt everything! My mind never left me once. And it was just us together, experiencing each other and loving each other. And then Gord went and got supper. We had Chinese food. Chinese food and candlelight. We sat for a while and just hugged and loved each other. And then we went to bed. He asked me why I had tears and I had tears of happiness because it feels so good. It felt so good to feel everything and to be with him. I felt like such a beautiful woman last night and I haven't felt like that in so long. I felt like a desirable, beautiful woman, and I loved myself last night.

I can't understand why I have tears when I'm happy. Since I met Gord, sometimes I have had tears of happiness almost as much as my tears of sadness before, and that is something I'm so thankful for. And now here I am again, crying because I'm happy about it. I can't help it. If I hadn't had to make the decision to face my abuse I don't know what I'd do or where I'd be now.

NOV. 15, '93

No One Can Decide for Us

Friday and Saturday were two of the best days I've had in the last ten months. I felt so carefree, and nothing worried me. I was alive, bright-eyed, joking and felt great. That's the feeling I want all the time. Relaxed, as well. Maybe one day it will come to stay. Then yesterday Gord was acting strange. I asked him about it, but he said it was nothing. I knew he was mad. That was the end of the good feeling for me. Finally, last night it came to a head, and I'm still mad today. I don't know how to get over it. I really haven't thought it through, and I didn't have much to say to him today at lunchtime.

I still feel the same tonight. Not much point in recording the whole episode because it's something I'd sooner just forget. I don't feel much like doing homework tonight, but I will do some to save beating myself up for it tomorrow. I'm really not looking forward to when he gets home; I'd sooner just be alone. He says he feels bad. What I got last night I did not deserve. This morning I felt like I was wasting my time doing all this. I do feel better about it now, but I don't feel very close to him tonight. It was both me and Jani; he got us both last night and she is scared. Just when the trust is going great—WHAM!

What did I do? I said no to something I didn't want to do and look what happened. You took good care of me this time, Janet. You didn't make me say sorry for something I didn't do, and you didn't say anything we have to feel bad about. We don't know yet about our dad and he can't decide for us. You did a good job keeping me away from him too. Gord doesn't think so but he'll never understand the way we do.

You are right, he never, never will, and that's unfortunate but we all have to try to help him. Sometimes it's hard to work so hard and then feel it's a waste of time, but the only way it would be is if we were doing it for him and we aren't. This is for you and me, don't ever forget that. Other people will benefit, but it's for us, Jani!

DEC. 04, '93

Tell Somebody Out Loud

I feel relieved that the night is over and that I don't have any new feelings that I haven't dealt with as far as my dad goes. I was dreading that tonight would bring up a lot of new things or a lot of... I don't know, horror, and it didn't. I feel good about that, and I feel like I put everything into tonight too. We were asked to speak about our offender and about our abuse if we wished to, and I did. Actually, when they said they wanted us to do that tonight it was like a great relief. Finally, I got to tell somebody out loud a little bit about it. I never really got into the actual physical part of what happened to me. I don't feel a need to do that, for me or for anyone else.

Then we did some exercises on the wall where we wrote different words and how they pertain to our abuse or our life now. Some of the words were threats, some were treats, one was humiliation, another was degradation, dependency, incompetence, and I can't remember what the others pertained to right now.

What else was there? Oh yes, isolation, aloneness—all different feelings about different times and different emotions that we had relating to the abuse. I was very afraid. It just goes to show you that you shouldn't worry about things before they happen, because it didn't happen. I think I can actually have a good sleep tonight. Next week is anger. I am going to make a point of trying to deal with some of that anger between now and next week's session. I'm going to approach it in a very honest way and see if I can't fish it up.

FOLLOWING DEC. 4, '93 (RECORDING)

Losing Touch

I find that I do have to do some work during the week. I didn't work last week, and I didn't work this week, but this coming week I am going to work because if I don't, I tend to lose touch with my feelings and with everything. I just lose touch with everything.

SOMETIME IN DEC. '93 OR JAN. '94

I Am Angry

If I was angry, I would throw things
If I was angry, I would act out violently
If I was angry, I would raise my voice
If I was angry, I would break things
If I was angry, I would say nothing
If I was angry, I would drink
If I was angry, I would clean things
If I was angry, I would hide it
If I was angry, I would go out

I am angry at you because you took away my childhood. I am angry at you because you treated me like crap, you totally controlled me, and you made sure I stayed that way for as long as possible. I am angry because I feel all the nice things I had as a child were tokens of "keep my mouth shut." I am angry that you treated my brother like he could never do anything right and I could never do anything wrong until I started rebelling against the abuse and then I could also do no right any longer.

Maybe that's why you treated Brad as you did all those years. He couldn't be so controlled by your sick mind. I am angry now as well for the things you did to me that are interfering with my life with Gord. We are both dealing with the abuse you handed out many years ago. I am also angry that you don't have the nerve to say a thing about it, and you can't be too dumb to know what's going on now. You are afraid to say anything to me and I enjoy watching you squirm at times. I know the truth and so do you. I am facing it. Can you?

JAN. 17, '94

Positive Changes

Changes Noticed – Positive – Since Healing Journey Began

- I don't grieve the abuse much anymore
- My life doesn't center around abuse anymore
- I can sleep through a whole night now without waking up or having nightmares
- I'm not afraid to go to sleep anymore
- I feel like part of my family
- My appetite is healthy
- I keep in touch with friends and family again
- I can laugh a lot again
- I can accept praise a lot better
- I no longer take pills to relax or sleep
- I no longer feel guilty about my abuse
- I gained a lot of self-esteem back
- I can connect and feel more consistently
- I can recognize it when I'm not connecting and feeling; still need work on getting back when I feel disassociated

- I like what I see in the mirror much more than dislike it
- I have a whole new relationship with my family now, within myself and without
- I can sympathize with myself now rather than get down on myself. This comes with ridding myself of guilt about abuse
- I can get in touch with the little girl inside who suffered the abuse and know she is part of me and it is she who suffers, not the adult me more so
- We have both, me and little Janet (Jani, as Gord calls her) learned to or are learning to accept our life as survivors rather than living in it. We both choose to accept and move on.

Areas We Need to Work With
- Communication about how I (we) are feeling about all things
- More exercise
- Form new relationships and deepen ones already formed
- Work on changing mindset and thoughts about sexual relationship, make it spontaneous again mentally, emotionally, physically
- Spend more time with my spiritual being, alone, searching inside to get in touch with who I am and my feelings

Janet, I haven't talked to you for a long time and I need to know how you are feeling, if you are all right and if you are getting as much benefit from this healing journey as I am.

Here I am. I've been sitting back taking it all in. I feel very different about myself now. I don't feel ugly and fat anymore like I used to. I feel more like a little girl again. Maybe I didn't get much chance to years ago, but I can remember a lot more kid things now. You help me to remember and you play with me now, but before you never did. I don't think you like me much. You were always trying to get rid of me. I could never understand why no one liked me. Now you sometimes do stuff with me. I loved it when we went skating and when we play with your kittens. I love it when you let Gord take care of us too. It feels like I have a whole new life. That was then, and this is now. I don't feel so alone anymore, and I am never afraid. I do wish we could be together more. We could be, if you'd let us. Just think about me more and we can do more things. You know, fun things, not so serious all the time. I can be serious at times, but it is easier to have fun and be there. I am happier now because you are my friend. You respect me, and you pay attention to me and you aren't mean to me. You always let me say anything I want about anything or anyone. You respect me.

I don't want you to take the first picture of me to your group. I don't feel comfortable with them seeing me like that, okay?

You want to honor me at your group celebration? You and Gord honor me lots now. I'm shy to have them hear what I say. I don't know what would be okay. You could tell them about me then and now if you want, would that be okay? You could still honor me but kind of keep our exact conversations private amongst our own. You tell them about me and I'll be honored. I'm having to go now. I like you, my new friend.

Janet, I am very happy and feel very warm about how comfortable you feel now. I am glad we can be friends and that you think I take good care of you. I do respect you and regret all the time we missed being together and all the time you were feeling so alone and afraid. For that I am sorry. I now have the ability to take care of you and be your friend. I think we can both be very thankful we have God, we have Gord and we have each other.

JAN. 20, '94 (RECORDING)

The Analogy

Last day of group. It's happy and it's sad. I feel warm inside and I feel like I've accomplished lots. I feel motivated to begin life maybe through the eyes of someone who wants to live, rather than somebody that is desperate, like I was so desperate, to heal. I still am, and there's a lot of work to do. One of the things that was talked about tonight was the fact that we have to stop thinking about life as healing by person to person and start healing the structure of life so that it doesn't continue, this constant bandaging of people. Find the people inflicting the wounds and fix the structure so that the wounds aren't inflicted anymore rather than bandaging, bandaging, bandaging.

Another thing that was stressed was the fact that the healing process for a survivor is the first step, and part of the healing process after you kind of get your proverbial blank together is to bring other people into the healing process and help them. And speak out against the war that's going on against women and children and do something about it. Become an activist, become political about it, start doing something about it. Help those that follow and help those that haven't dealt with surviving yet.

There was a lot of sadness tonight amongst people in the group. It was a relieved sadness that it was over, but a sadness that we'd be leaving the comfort of sharing with each other and the group closeness that everyone felt.

I know even our leaders were teary-eyed tonight. The only things I really got teary-eyed about were some of the things people shared. I watched one of my group members burn the picture of her offender in the fire tonight. There was a lot of emotion in the room and it felt good because everyone there had been through this journey together. One of our leaders told us about the woman who was in a bare and desolate land and couldn't get warm. She covered up with so many blankets of clothing and lived alone and didn't know what it was like to feel warm and laugh and dance and share. A voice came to the door and told her to come out. She had to leave that room or perish, and she left with that stranger feeling comfortable. As they travelled along the road the barren trees became green, and she shed the clothing and soon she found herself dancing and singing and enjoying life.

It was really an analogy to the healing process, and I just thought it was so neat. It was like "yes, that's me." And all the emotion in that room tonight was great because a lot of us went there feeling nothing or were just learning how to feel, and everybody felt for everybody else and everybody felt for themselves tonight and it was a real sign of progress that we made there. When we got back from listening to the lecture, just as I was leaving, one particular group member pulled up in the street and came up and said, "Well ..." and we just put our arms around each other and it was kind of like "We'll see you, and I'll really miss you," and we exchanged phone numbers.

I also look forward to being able to speak out one day with my story to someone who needs to hear it or to someone who might need my help to get through. Because it is a struggle, and as our group leaders explained in their lecture tonight, there is a definite war in the world against women and children, and something has got to be done about it. I don't know what. Perhaps one day I will put all my notes together and hopefully lend it to someone or give it to someone that is either going through the same thing or intends to help someone else with it. I guess that will be my way of being public with my story; it can be used to help others. Maybe, maybe not. Maybe it will help some caregiver gain insight into the life of a survivor and the different things that they go through in their mind. I really don't know what else to say or where I'll go from here, but I do consider it a most beneficial move on my part to go to group. I've been extremely fortunate to find Susan and my group leaders. They are very supportive and very positive about the healing process. I'm so thankful to the women in my group for sharing their stories and letting me learn from them and letting me be a part of their healing process.

It's unbelievable the strength that is in that room, actually, when you stop and think about it, and I used to think it was weakness, but there's a lot of strength in that room because we have all survived and we're all trying to help ourselves. I've built a certain kind of relationship with them in that group. One thing I know I can say is I'm proud of us all!

JAN. 24, '94

Feeling Very Confident

I am feeling very confident these days. My new job promotion has been great for my self-esteem and self-worth. In areas where I am struggling, it's nice to know I have still got what it takes to be a leader and I was chosen for this job because they believe I am a leader and more than capable of making responsible decisions that are in the best interest of the company. I have full support from those above me and from most beside me.

Gord and I and some friends curled in the mixed bonspiel this past weekend. I felt alive, I had fun!! I enjoyed being around people.

Tonight, I was home alone until 8:30 p.m. I shaved my legs, did my nails and had a shower. Sometimes I feel like I need more time to myself than two-and-a-half hours a week. I don't know how to get it, though. I'll have to come up with some kind of plan that will work for Gord too.

OCT. 17, '95

Keep the Children Safe

I went to see Susan last night, drove home and immediately picked up the phone and called Brad. I've broken the silence AGAIN! I told him about being sexually abused by Dad so that Brad could keep the children safe. It took all I had.

Today I feel like I've been run over by a train. I called Susan today and she said I've done exceptionally well and I should be very proud of myself for how far I've come and how I've had a relationship to work with at the same time. She said she had no idea I'd go "gung ho" when I left there last night and go straight home and do it. She is very happy for me and says what I'm feeling is "shock." She says when the shock passes I'll feel much lighter and that it's such great timing too, for Brad's sake. He goes for stress psychology next month and I told him last night to spill his guts; it's done me wonders, and if I was abused there's no way he wasn't in some form or another.

He seemed to be in shock too, but he told me he was proud of me, he loved me, and he couldn't find the exact words he wanted to say to me just then, but we'll talk again on Friday. I'm sad that Brad too will most likely have to go through such anger, but it's part of a healthy process. Susan says this whole thing could add years to Brad's life because I've come clean with him, shown him it can be done, and he is supporting me. I am still in shock. I still can't believe I've done it, but those little children can't have to go through what I have. Life is too great and I'm only just finding that out. There's no way I could have the strength on my own to do all of this without God and without Gord. It's true, I don't know anymore where I'd be.

MARCH 31, '97

You're Protecting Them, Aren't You?

I feel myself slipping back into a shell. The last six to eight months or more I've become shallow and extremely stressed by the littlest things. Depression and stress are ruling my life once more. Chiropractic visits, insomnia, low sex drive and the urge to go away are always somewhere. Gord and I went to see Susan last Thursday and she says it's par for the course. I worked, I worked hard, I worked fast, and now comes a different level. Anger seems to be the culprit. It's built up inside again. She says I now need to release it, and I agree with her. It's my inner child who is suffering again. I need to find out why. I've be neglecting her big time. I feel like a pressure cooker, and the lid's about to blow.

Janet, are you there? I know I haven't found you in a long time. It's been too long since you've been free to play, free to scream, free to say what you need to say.

I'm confused. So confused. Sometimes I hate my dad. I want for both of them to say they're sorry. That's what I want. If they could, I would be okay. I'm tired of pretending nothing happened. Everyone knows it did, but no one will ever say anything.

Janet, do you want to say something? Do you want to bring it up? What if he makes you feel guilty again, what if he denies it, pretends it wasn't how it was? What if he threatens us, cuts us off from his life? What if he... whatever?

You know. I know. Gord knows. Susan knows. My mind is racing. I don't know what I want. I thought it was you who didn't want to say anything. I'm mixed up. I can't think. I'm a little girl who can't have fun again. I want to. I deserve to. We were for a while. What happened?

Janet, I don't know. Somehow you slipped away from me. I slipped away from you. I need to be able to laugh again at silly things, be creative and goofy, be free. I'm sorry. I can't help you today. I can't dig back far enough.

A friend phoned and is worried about you and you can't even say what's wrong. You're ashamed, aren't you? Are you ashamed of me or yourself? You're holding out.

You have to tell. You're protecting them, aren't you? You don't want anyone else to know that your family isn't who they seem.

I'm not ashamed of you, Janet. You were a helpless, controlled child. I do not hold you responsible for what happened. Maybe I am ashamed of myself for not being able to let go of this thing. What do I do, how do I get over it? How do I go on?

I can't bring myself to ruin someone else's life because mine isn't right. He did it to me, and revenge isn't my bag. Would I be a better person for bringing him to his knees? I don't feel I would be.

Janet, you and I need to talk; you're a mess.

It seems that you're trying to take care of me now. Maybe I need that. You are right. I am and thank you for being there.

APRIL 3, '97

We Can't Run Anymore

My depression has gotten worse. Too much responsibility! It's little Janet, I think, that is retaliating. She doesn't
want any responsibility. She's had to have way too much.
She's never had the chance not to have any. She's always
had major pressure, major responsibility, major secrets
and way too much to contain for one person.

Until I free her somehow, someway, I'll struggle forever. I know as an adult I have almost everything. A
loving husband, a beautiful home, friends, a great job.
What more could I ask for? Sexual freedom and peace of
mind are the missing components. Somehow, we need
to come to some kind of compromising agreement. Why
is she so difficult when it comes to responsibility? Is it
a control issue? Is that the only thing she feels she can
control? Or is that the adult me that feels that way? Why
the necessity for everything to be just so? It's not her or
my responsibility. Let it go. Let it go. Let it go.

I don't like having any interference in my life caused by other people. I've had enough. I don't need any other garbage in my life. Before, I could just leave it behind and forget but I'll never be able to. Your first husband was kind and thoughtful, but we didn't want the same things. He was happy in the present, and I couldn't be. He didn't know what he was married to and I wasn't ready to tell. A couple of your boy-friends were alright for a while, but they either drank too much too and reminded me in that way of my dad or they wouldn't call and had too many family issues, and that took too much of my energy and theirs. Dad, I hated him so much that sometimes I hit him. He thought he knew what love was, but he had no clue. You picked another because you thought he was the thing to do. Decent job, talked the talk. He would lie and tell you what you wanted to hear. That must have been a weak point in your life! And then he cheated on you with someone who befriended you—not the best judge of character there, Janet. Again, when things got too much, we could walk away. This time we can't. Now we have Gord. We could do whatever we wanted with-out any discomfort in our lives. No interfering family, no outside chaos, we could move to South America, but we've never had a Gord. We can't run anymore.

Here we are. If we could only find a way to keep others'

garbage from getting to us, draw distinct boundaries. We don't need anyone else. How are we going to do that? We can't run anymore. We are here now; we have to deal. Before, we didn't. We have to find out how. I don't know, do you?

Oh Janet, I think you're right. We do have to find out how to accept, let go of these things, those outside interferences, negative and disturbed people. We can't change them. We have to change. We can't run anymore. You're right. We, I, you, screwed up before and made the choices we did for whatever reasons but when we had enough it was easy to walk away.

We both are about to learn a big lesson in life we never had to before. We had to stay with Dad, but that was because we would never have made it on our own. We were too young, too inexperienced about life. Now we can't run for other reasons. Gord is part of our life and will always be. We want him to be. What do we do about the rest? Our discomfort with family and the legal crap, the carry-over it creates. Neither of us have it in us, and probably never will, to accept such chaos and live with it. Our family. The secrecy, the manipulation, the guilt, the shame, the tension, the love, the need for them even after what happened to us. How do we deal with all of it when we can't run anymore?

We need help!!

JULY 6, '99

Worst Fear Confirmed, Police and Lawyers

(WARNING: GRAPHIC AND VIOLENT)

Finally!! The worst is over, and the world didn't end. On June 27, the phone rings after 10:00 p.m. It's Brad; he's livid. He says he's got a gun and he's going to the farm to give him what he deserves. He tells me many things. He tells me to be an honest person and to tell the truth. Dad abused me and it's time to face it. He also tells me he was abused by Dad. We talk, we hang up, I call back. Mom gets on the phone and says, "Brad told me Dad did terrible things to you kids when you were little. Is it true?"

I say, "Yes." Mom is crying, and I talk to her for a while. I speak to Brad and make him promise not to go to the farm because he has a family to think about and our dad isn't worth the consequences. I phone our dad at the farm and tell him Brad is coming out there. He asks what for. I say, "Something that should have been taken care of thirty years ago." I tell him if he knows what's good for him, he'll make sure Brad does not get hurt.

He says, "If you think I'm going to stand here and let him beat the piss out of me, I am not."

I tell him, "Make sure nothing happens to Brad" and hang up. I phone back Brad and Mom at Mom's place in town and Brad has agreed to stay away from the farm. We talk for a long time and Brad confirms my worst fear. I feel all the hate come over me again. Not him too!! The three of us talk and Brad says not to come. Gord won't let me leave that night.

I left the next morning at 7:30 a.m. Monday July 28, '99. I phoned and left a message for Susan to please call me on my cell. My boss told me to do what I need to do to take care of my family. I phoned Brad as well and told him to get Mom to the bank to get cash out before she can't. I go to Brad's. Mom has stayed there. We talk, we hug, we cry together. We go to Mom's and do more of the same. Brad goes home. The phone rings. I answer, and it's dad.

"What are you doing there?" he says.

I say, "I'm here talking care of business."

"What business?" he asks.

My reply is the same, "Something that should have been done thirty years ago." Mom picks up the other phone. She does not want to talk to him, but she listens.

I tell him we are sick and tired and don't want him in our lives anymore. He has controlled us, abused us, and it's over. He denies and plays stupid. I tell him he sexually abused me from ages nine to sixteen and he abused Brad too. I don't recall now when or how often. He denies it. Calls me a liar, calls Brad a liar. I tell him to shut up and listen, and this is how it's going to be. He leaves and gives us what we want. He says I'll get nothing. I tell him I don't want anything from him, never have, and never will. Brad doesn't want anything from him either, but Mom will get whatever she wants, and she'll be looked after. He denies it again and I say, "You sexually abused me, did you or did you not?"

He says, "Yes, but I never touched Brad!"

Mom's mouth drops. She believed us but needed to hear it from him. He did not know she was listening. I tell him if it were Brad on the phone confronting him he would say, "Yes, I did, but I never touched your sister."

I tell him again to stay away, and that he'd better look after Mom. He says. "I've got to live too." I say we don't care about him. He asks when we'll have a list. I say later and hang up.

He phones back later in the afternoon and demands to talk to Mom. She is on the other line. I tell him there is a houseful, and nobody wants him there. He says he'll come and kick us all out. Mom then has something to say. He asks her if she is going along with this garbage.

She says it is garbage and she heard him say on the phone earlier that he sexually abused me. I am listening. He tells her he did it once, but he was drunk. She tells him that once is too often and the rest I don't recall because I started calling him a liar and verbally degrading him and then I cut him off.

That night, Mom and I stayed there. I put a knife in the shoes in the porch, locked the doors, and put a chair under the knob. The next morning, he showed up and pushed his way into the house. We heard him upstairs, quickly got dressed and when we got there he was at the table eating cereal. I asked him if this was Plan C. He called me a name and told me to keep my mouth shut. Well, that didn't happen. He called me a bad name again and told me that Gord told him he was going to dump me because I was such a B word. This is how mean he could be, how cruel. I told him to get out and called him all kinds of names. He told me to get out and I told him I'd fix him. He grabbed me by the sweater and a fight followed. He slapped me and tried to knock me down. I held him, and Mom was trying to get him to let go. When I finally let go, it was only because Mom was screaming at him, he dropped me to the floor in the porch the minute my hands came off his shirt. I landed on my back with him on top of me. I tried to kick him to get him to let me go. He let me up and said he'd leave. He didn't. He went upstairs to change his clothes. I waited in the kitchen. My finger was bleeding and my arms hurt. My foot was bleeding and cut.

He changed his shirt and took Mom's car. He said he'd bring it back. I told her not to give it to him, but I couldn't defend myself against him again, so she let him have it. I told him I hoped he died.

We went to the police and the lawyer that day. The police wanted me to press assault charges, but I told them I did not care to ever see him again and I wasn't wasting any more of my life on him in court or any-where else. I did tell them I would if it meant getting a restraining order for my mom. They said, and so did the lawyer, that it wasn't necessary. They had enough to get one without that. I wish now that I had pressed charges.

Mom and I stayed at Brad's till Thursday. It's terrible to again be afraid of someone who has already stolen a large part of your life and then laughed in your face about it.

I feel bad for Mom. I feel bad for Brad. All our father was worried about was getting the list of demands we wanted in exchange for not putting his name in every paper from here to the east coast. He'd better produce, because Brad and I are on the very edge of blowing him out of the water and splashing his name all over the place as a sexual abuser and a child molester.

The lawyer he has would be surprised to hear he's representing a child molester with no remorse, wouldn't he? If I have to, I'll tell him. My lawyer knows and the RCMP corporal was also told he has been an abuser of all kinds for many years.

Do I feel bad for him being all alone with leukemia? I may have if his reaction had been what we deserved. Right now, I do not. He'll be judged, he'll have to deal alone, either on this Earth or after. He's the one who doused himself in gas and kept lighting the match time and time again instead of getting help. He is heartless, has no remorse and deserves absolutely nothing from me.

Mom better get what she has coming, or I'll put an article in every newspaper possible about what a perverted, denying child molester he is. His lawyer may need to hear about it. The threat of a civil suit may just do it. I'll keep those cards for now and play them if I have to. He owes her everything. He did a horrible, heinous thing, not only to her children, but to her. I don't even think I hate him now for what he's done to me or his reaction to me, because Susan helped prepare me for that, but to know that the abuse happened to Brad too and how Mom must feel now...

This is not a matter of 50-50 anymore. It's a matter of him getting what he well deserves. "Please God have mercy on my family and teach this man the lessons of life while he is still on this Earth or take him and teach him wherever you see fit to put him. Amen".

FOLLOWING JULY OF '99
Life and Death Go On

After much going back and forth, and I can't imagine what all, my parents got back together, lived together and remained married.

One day as I was sitting on the deck at our home, I recall opening an envelope that had come in the mail. There in black and white was a letter from my father asking for forgiveness for what he had done. Today it's still in my safe deposit box; it hasn't been read since I received it all those years ago.

In the fall of 2001, a long-time friend told me about a program that changed her life. It's called Choices.* I went. There are no words to explain to you how that changed my life! It's now years later and the life experience I had there is even more monumental and pivotal to me now than I can describe.

So, on my drive back home from Calgary, I called Brad and told him that he must go. Please, I said. And he does.

* choicesseminars.com

Again, it is life-changing for him. Then Gord and my parents went after that. What goes on in there is always held in high confidence, so I cannot tell you about their experiences, but I know for our family it was of major importance in the times to come.

Gord and I, finally, after raising his son, decided it was time to get married and so we had a small family and few close friends come to our wedding on September 6, 2003. I don't recommend waiting twelve years. All the members of our immediate families were present. Gord and I had decided we wanted to get married while all our family members were still alive to attend. His dad had been ill on and off.

In May of 2004, Gord's dad died in the hospital during what should have been and is mainly a routine blood transfusion. This man had survived so many major medical issues in the past, and it was difficult to believe that he just closed his eyes peacefully and died that day with no notice, with no medical interventions to bring him back as there had been prior; it was just peaceful and quiet. I will never forget that peace that came over me when I walked into that hospital room and saw his body lying there. It was like seeing live, in person, God's promise that our spirit leaves the body, and nothing is left but the tent. If I wasn't smiling, it was out of pure consideration for Gord and his mom. Molly remained the ever-strong mom through those weeks. I recall her saying, "I'm still your mom" when one of us was having a sad time as we were making funeral plans.

In the meantime, we believed my father's cancer surgery had been successful back in November of 2003, but his cancer had come back with vengeance. The day after Gord's dad's funeral, we went home and slept and then went to Bow Island where my dad lay dying. The cancer was in his bones and progressing throughout his body. God used those days hugely to show His mercy and grace for all of us. My brother and my mom were out of his room when I realized undoubtedly that Dad was taking his final breaths. The nurse went down the hall to get my mom and I was beside him when he drew that final breath and silence filled the room. So many things came to me in that few minutes. It was only with the miracle of God's forgiveness, which had taken place in the years prior, that I could have been there and experienced God's presence in such a tangible way. It was like if I could have reached inside of my dad I could have touched God. I could feel His presence and it was so powerful and so emblazoned in my mind and heart, yet I can not explain it. It sounds strange; I know the last chapter was about telling my dad I wanted him to die, and now you are reading this. Only God can create miracles in hearts and in moments like these. He had done a work in our family that no worldly person or idol or anyone, for that matter, could have done. Was it perfect? NO! Was it healing? Yes!

Were we happily ever after? NO! Were we a family that had worked on it and come to a place where we could have a relationship, each with their own boundaries that we could, for the most part, live with? Yes!

So not even two weeks following Walter's (Gord's dad) death, my dad died. It was difficult watching him for many days knowing there was no hope for healing here on Earth. It was difficult to face the fact that not so long ago, I had wished him dead. It was difficult to watch my family and friends go through this process of watching my dad die. Yet for me it was a time of realization of how far we had come, how much forgiveness there was, regardless of what we had all endured in the past few years. I am not writing this to have you think we became the model family or the envy of anyone, but to let you know that in spite of the horrendous things that had taken place when my brother and I were children and teens, the damage and loss that came with it as adults, the enemy didn't win!! He couldn't destroy us in life and he couldn't destroy us in death.

And so the following months were filled with caring for our moms and being there when we could. Fortunately for me, I had left my full-time work and was able to be where I needed to be without the added responsibility of being committed otherwise. That is another story of great timing, which I may write about another time. Gord was in the midst of changing jobs after thirty-two years and was due to start his new one on or about the middle week of August 2004. And then the phone call came on August 11, 2004.

It was my mom telling me that Brad, my brother, was dead ... it was like something out of the twilight zone. How could this be happening? We had just lost our dads in May, and now ten weeks later my brother?! I recall it was late at night and although I wanted to get to my mom as soon as possible, it didn't make any feasible sense for us to drive or for me to go alone, travelling in the night. And so the next day, Gord and I went to Mom's. It was all a blur, truthfully. We went into funeral-planning mode, and that kept me sane most of the days. My desire for a cigarette and alcohol, my old coping methods, came up again. I cannot to this day decipher the difference between my dad's funeral and my brother's except that the music was different, of course, and there were some different people there. But who was where, I can't tell you. I do know the faces of the people that made the time to come. I can name them off to you and I cannot tell you how each one of them was appreciated for simply being there! If you have had a funeral in your family you know how each heart that extends itself to be present for you, calls you, or shows up is never forgotten.

This was too much for me. When I returned home, I recall days that I could not get out of my chair. I would cry at the very thought that there was dirty laundry that had to be addressed. My biggest fear was, "Will I ever get my joy back?" I had worked so hard dealing with my past abuse and had come to a place that I was free and joyful, and now this!

It was logical, to my mind, that our fathers had died, even though it was before their time. It made sense in our world that our parents went before us. But now my brother was dead of a massive heart attack—the third heart attack we were aware of. There was no worldly place or person that could fix this for me. As I sat at home in my own grief, I had a choice to make yet again: do I fight now and recover all I have worked for or do I accept where I am in this sad, empty dark place and become one of the walking, breathing dead? It's like I had come to a place where I had no place to go except to God! And I knew it.

It took everything I had to open my Bible. I was mad at God. How could He have let this happen? After all our family had been through, fought to recover and lost, now my brother?! I was so angry at God some days that I would swear out loud at Him, and now to realize He was the answer to my future was difficult to swallow. Even though at times I felt like hiding my Bible in the drawer or even yanking it apart into tiny pieces, He gave me the grace and the strength to open it. It was my joy I feared I would lose permanently, so I searched the verses, the promises in the Bible regarding joy.

It was a process. It was hard work, it was some days putting one foot in front of another begrudgingly. But I refused to roll over and die and let the enemy have any more ground in my life than he had tried to take in the past. Now the war was on! I got determined and I got mad, and I decided I was going to live by the promises of God and not the death and destruction of the enemy in the world, that I was going to be a victor and not a victim and that there was no way in hell I would do anything but! I would have my joy back in spite of my losses and no one was going to stop me! And I would do all in my power to take my mom to this place as well. We were left, and we were going to be an example for other people, not of giving up on life, but of living it to the fullest in spite of life AND death!

It was by happenchance, one might say, but a miracle to me, in fact, that I found Ronna Jevne, PhD, who agreed to help me in my grief. Google her.* You will see why she is remarkable. As well as being a registered psychologist, author and photographer, she is a founding member of the Hope Foundation of Alberta (now Hope Studies Central) and a founding member of CAPO (the Canadian Association of Psychosocial Oncology). She also has a passion for encouraging writing as a way

---

* Her old website is ronnajevne.ca. The Prairie Wind website is prairiewindwritingcentre.ca

of recovering and sustaining our mental health. Her newest endeavour, with her husband, is the Prairie Wind Writing Centre. She was and is another great example in my life of the promise that you get double for your trouble. And I felt like I had had all the trouble I could possibly handle. After much grace and hard heart work and prayer, I can say that the joy I regained following these deaths is greater than that I had achieved prior.

I so distinctly recall how worried Molly, (my mother-in-law) was about me. Even though she was going through the grief of losing Walter, she remained a mom to me, always until the last of her days. It was apparent to our family that when Walter died, Molly either couldn't or didn't want to go on without him. There is no way to describe the gift of time spent with her leading up to her time in the hospital and her time in there. I just couldn't imagine myself being anywhere else, and God provided the most loving and caring nurses for her and the most meaningful conversations and sharing of time and space that either of us could have made up. Molly passed away on the evening of June 16, 2005. It was a huge loss for us. The family matriarch sounds so cliché, but she was the epitome. She created the family dinners, gave the strong and understanding advice, and remained the mom to her last breath. The gift of having Molly and Walter as in-laws in one of the biggest gifts in my lifetime! They accepted me, treated me as one their own, and respected me as Gord's wife and the kid's stepmom. They loved me unconditionally, and I loved them the same! We had no history, just who we were when we met and who we all grew to be in the years that we got to share. I will be forever grateful.

JULY 3, '08

A Place of Extraordinary Meaning

As I walk the tarmac from the terminal to the plane, I look out over the desert and feel the intense heat of the past days in a way that I've never felt it before. As the breeze softly blows over me, I stand for a short time and take it all in. As I board the Dash 8, I feel as if I'm leaving a place that holds extraordinary meaning to me. Not until I'm seated and buckled in do I get the depth of what I'm experiencing. The prop is going right outside my window and as I stare out, tears start to fall slowly down my cheeks. I've had moments of pride in my accomplishments before, but this is different; it is like a true revelation, an instant in time when all things seem to carry forward in a different perspective following it. I think, "You've come a long way, Janet, from that little girl on the prairie. The little girl with attitude, the little girl that was abused, the little girl that fought back to become what she is today." My tears were for her, for her fight, for what she's been through, but mostly for what she has managed to become.

I don't think I'll ever forget that feeling. I can see the desert so vividly, feel the intense, hot breeze in my face, and recall that quiet, almost overwhelming peace of realization. It seemed like no one else existed; just me with my thoughts. It's easy sometimes to say or think we've done an exceptional job or that we were successful at one thing or another, but it was staring out the window of that plane that I truly felt and knew instinctively just how much I'd overcome!

NEW YEAR 2018

Epilogue

Here we are now in the winter of 2018. We have been settled for a few months in our home in Arizona. This will mark our tenth year here.

Our families' lives, thankfully, have for the most part been filled with stories of growth, healing, adventure and answers to prayer, some of which have been many, many years in the making. And there are more we are waiting on.

Through the deaths of our family members, God used those experiences to prepare me and to fire up a long-ago desire I had to one day work at a funeral home. And I did, part time for about four years. I met many wonderful people there and it was a joy for me to be able to help in any little way those people who were dealing with the loss of their loved one. I drove the coach (the hearse), seated people at services, helped them take care of paperwork and preplanned funerals, but most of all was able to love on them, period. Seeing and being involved in death so much over that period made a huge difference in how I view life and prioritize my time. It is short, it must be meaningful, and most of all, it really isn't all about us! Life is about relationships, living in truth, and how we impact others lives.

For the past thirteen years, I have been a volunteer Victim Services Advocate with the Royal Canadian Mounted Police. Each time we get a referral or answer a call it is a pivotal space in time where we as advocates have an opportunity to help people. Our goals are to deliver intervention, give referrals and supply information. There is no better way to describe it, in my estimation, than to say we serve. We serve by intervening and using our training, both academic and experiential, to help people in what can be the most devastating, life-altering crisis in their lives. Perhaps as you read this book, my story comes to you in a critical time, gives you information, or acts as an intervention to go head to head with your past and prompt you to fight for the life that you were created for and so deserve.

It's my heart's desire to see all lives changed by acknowledging the truth of what has happened in the past, so we can all be unrestricted to carry on in the future in freedom, to be true to who God created us to be! And not who the enemy has worked so diligently to make us think we are... damaged, unusable, unseen, unheard, unloved. Those are all lies.

Years ago, when I joked about being "on a mission from God," I had no idea I actually really and truly would be. He has taken all that's been meant for my destruction and used it for His good purposes in a broken world. Yes, He will use the least of us.

And so, I leave you with my story and pray that in some way you have found hope in it, that it brings you an awareness of how you don't have to accept life based on whatever bad circumstances you have had or are having, and that yes, life does happen to us all. However, there is hope! There is a better way to live out your days than accepting what the world throws at you. Know that yes, there is an enemy that wants to destroy you, BUT God is bigger than all those horrible things that happen to us and others in the world, and He will use them to grow you and prosper you if you allow it.

Our family legacy isn't about abuse or about a broken family. It is one of strength, courage, perseverance and forgiveness. It is about deliverance. It is about sharing our story so that others can find HOPE in it! Hope in the darkest of situations, hope in the midst of fighting for your life, hope that brings healing to the soul, the HOPE of Jesus who we cried out to and who has led us to this moment. The darkness is no more. There is nowhere for the enemy to hide his deceitful, lying, low-life, dead and destroying schemes. No! When exposed to the light, all that the enemy throws at us to keep us from living our

God-given life and purpose is obliterated and wasted on us. Instead, we go on to share and to help others see light. Look up, reach up!

How can you change the trajectory of your life? Acknowledge your pain. Others may have inflicted it on you and it was out of your control, you yourself may have made big mistakes based on your past, or made bad choices based on what you did or didn't know. We all have done it and we all need a place of peace and forgiveness. I encourage you, I beg you, to reach out for help. Find a counsellor, psychologist, support group, someone who is an expert in this field. Life is so bright and wonderful when you no longer live in the past or the present with your pain, whatever has caused it. Please don't continue through life concealing your pain and masking it. At the end of this book you will find a list of references to help, and some are generic, based on the area in which you live. They are places you can start if you don't know where to turn.

I do not suggest or endorse in any way that if you are a believer of any kind in God you do not also seek the professional help and resources that have been put in the world for you. I have seen too many believers stuck in the past and living a less than fulfilling life because they refuse the help and resources that are available to them outside of the church. Some may require medication prescribed by a professional and caring health-care provider in addition to counsel for a time, some may require in-hospital or outpatient care, others may need individual psychiatric care, counseling by a professional who deals with your subject matter, and/or group therapy. I encourage you to use the resources available to you. Life is meant to be bright and exciting!

You can also change the trajectory of your life, if you choose to and haven't already done so, by asking Jesus to come into it. Maybe this will be the first time, or maybe you have walked away in the past. This is not an overnight miracle; it's a lifetime miracle. And once you do it, you will understand. It's not necessary to shave your head and hang out in the airport to make a statement. It's simply about living a life that you have asked Jesus for help with. It certainly can't make it any worse, can it? Well, there may be people who forsake you. You may lose some people you thought were friends, but don't worry about that! They have their path they are on and you can love them from the distance they are comfortable with. And you will make new friends, and new habits and have direction in your life that comes from the ONE who created it. If this is what you would like for your life, read the prayer at the end of the chapter out loud, believe it and seek the life that Jesus was an example of and is! Get a Bible and begin reading in the book of John or Luke. This isn't about religion or about what church you were raised in. It's not about what denomination you belong to or getting involved in anything strange or unusual. It's simply about having a personal relationship with Jesus Christ. You will begin to experience life and changes that no one on Earth can fulfill for you. You will begin to see, in new ways, who you were created to be and the truth of who you are! Your saviour in all dim and life-threatening situations, past, present and future, is Jesus. He is real, He is love and He is waiting for you.

And know that by this testimony, God is no respecter of persons. This means He doesn't love me more than you, He doesn't love you more than the next person.... He wants the best for ALL of us! If He did it for me, He will do it for you. Roll up your sleeves and choose life!!

Salvation Prayer:

God, I thank you for your love and your grace as you sent your only begotten Son to die as the sacrifice to pay the price for the sins of all humankind. I respond today to your love for me personally and I confess that I have sin in my life. I believe that you died for my sin and that you and you alone can forgive sin. I ask that you forgive me and that my sin would be removed from me as far as the east is from the west. I thank you that as you have forgiven me my name is now written in the Lamb's Book of Life. I pray that you will heal my heart and repair my brokenness as I make you the Lord of my life. Amen.

Prayer provided by Pastor Deborah Daniels

Psalm 56:8-13 The Voice

8 You have taken note of my journey through life,
  caught each of my tears in Your bottle.
  But God, are they not also blots on Your book?
9 Then my enemies shall turn back and scatter
  on the day I call out *to You*.
  This I know for certain: God is on my side.
10 In God whose word I praise
  and in the Eternal whose word I praise—
11 In God I have placed my trust. I shall not let fear come in,
  for what can measly men do to me?
12 I am bound by Your promise, O God.
  My life is my offering of thanksgiving to You,
13 For You have saved my soul from the darkness of death,
  steadied my feet from stumbling
 So I might continue to walk before God,
  embraced in the light of the living.

For this I am ever grateful and forever in AWE. All of the glory goes to you Father, Son and Holy Spirit.

Helpful References

Contact the organization closest to your area:
- Police department
- Victim Services Unit
- Check your area directory for a list of psychologists, counselors and professionals in the area specific to your experience
- Sexual assault center
- Social service agency
- Hospital
- Mental health center
- Distress center
- Community service organizations that provide counsel to adults, children and family
- Child and Family Services

Helpful websites:

www.littlewarriors.ca
Little Warriors is a national, charitable organization committed to awareness, prevention and treatment of child sexual abuse.

www.sexassault.ca

www.sexassault.ca/statistics.htm

www.rainn.org/articles/adult-survivors-child-sexual-abuse

www.rainn.org/articles/warning-signs-young-children

www.choicesseminars.com

www.luciac.com/recovery-of-your-inner-child

Acknowledgments

Thank you to:

My husband Gord, the first person I told, who has always supported me, stood by me, encouraged me, given me a safe place to become who I am, and most of all shared his love and his life with me. We have so much more to come.

My brother, Brad, who had the courage to step out with the truth.

My father, who did the best he knew how in the end to make amends and apologize.

Susan and Thelma, who helped us find our peace.

Vicki and Leslie—my encounters with each of you made it all worthwhile.

My mom, who could have made choices based on what other people said and who made difficult decisions before, during and after that have led us to this space in time. And most of all for being a praying mom.

Printed in Canada